THINK TANK LIBRARY

# CAVEAT!

*By 1998 neuroscientists could use positron emission tomography to observe and measure the elasticity of the developing brain, along with the rate of what is technically called synaptogenesis!*

In plain English that means scientists are now able to measure brain development. In fact, they have evidence showing that children ages 4 to 10 generate new brain synapses at a rate double that of adults and this young glucose-rich brain physiology is ideal for growth.

This should be a warning to elementary teachers and librarians in no uncertain terms: Carpe diem! Now is the time when opportunity knocks! *Children are ready to use their rapid cerebral glucose metabolism to think, to hard wire new knowledge, and understand their world.*

Chugani, Harry. "A Critical Period of Brain Development: Studies of Cerebral Glucose Utilization with PET." *Preventive Medicine* 7 (1998): 184–188. (And many other scientists subsequently.)

# THINK TANK LIBRARY

## BRAIN-BASED LEARNING PLANS FOR NEW STANDARDS, GRADES K–5

*Paige Jaeger and Mary Boyd Ratzer*

**LIBRARIES UNLIMITED**

AN IMPRINT OF ABC-CLIO, LLC
Santa Barbara, California • Denver, Colorado • Oxford, England

**Library of Congress Cataloging-in-Publication Data**

Jaeger, Paige.
   Think tank library : brain-based learning plans for new standards, grades K-5 / Paige Jaeger and Mary Boyd Ratzer.
      pages cm
   Includes bibliographical references and index.
      ISBN 978–1–61069–990–7 (paperback) — ISBN 978–1–61069–991–4 (ebook)  1. School libraries—United States. 2. School librarian participation in curriculum planning—United States. 3. Inquiry-based learning—United States. 4. Education—Standards—United States. 5. Thought and thinking—Study and teaching (Elementary)—United States.  I. Ratzer, Mary Boyd. II. Title.
   Z675.S3J235   2015
   027.80973—dc23            2014027779

ISBN: 978–1–61069–990–7
EISBN: 978–1–61069–991–4

19 18 17 16 15      1 2 3 4 5

This book is also available on the World Wide Web as an eBook.
Visit www.abc-clio.com for details.

Libraries Unlimited
An Imprint of ABC-CLIO, LLC

ABC-CLIO, LLC
130 Cremona Drive, P.O. Box 1911
Santa Barbara, California 93116-1911

This book is printed on acid-free paper ∞

Manufactured in the United States of America

# CONTENTS

# ACKNOWLEDGMENTS

Thank you to the professional organizations that gave permission to use their essential frameworks and guidance: NCSS, NCTE, and CAST UDL

The following colleagues who contributed lesson ideas or lesson pilot feedback for this book. This field testing and field contribution adds to the strength of the content. This showcases the cooperative resources-sharing characteristic for which our profession is known.

## CONTRIBUTORS AND FIELD TESTERS

Lauren Abad, Librarian, Greenfield Elementary School, Saratoga Springs City School District, contributor, Put Me in the Zoo.

Laurie Alden, Librarian, Harrison Avenue Elementary, South Glens Falls whose "Wonder Grid" was modified and included as a questioning tool.

Liz Bailey, Librarian Teacher, and Karen Robbins, Grade 3 Teacher, submitted their World Scrapbook idea, which was field-tested and modified, simplified, for use in the third grade.

Ann Marie Bilodeau, Argyle Central K-12 Librarian, Argyle, NY—field tester and contributor.

Liz Clancy, and kindergarten teachers of the Gordon Creek Elementary School, Ballston Spa Central Schools, NY. (Karen Benson, Deb Hodgson, Stacey Walz, Karen Smiley, Jacqui Kotula, Tracy Smith, Sharee Covelle, and Andrea Williams, librarian.)

Steve Danna, PhD, Dean of Branch Campus, SUNY Plattsburgh at Queensbury—Colleague and local Brain Research advocate.

Laura Gagnon, Elementary Librarian, Radez Elementary School, Cobleskill NY contributed her Battle of Cobleskill Unit. This unit was presented at the Annual Inquiry Forum, facilitated by Mary Ratzer, at the Hudson Valley Community College.

Carrie Giacobbe, Librarian, Granville Central Schools, field-tester.

Stacie Jaeger, Teacher, Spa Christian School, Ballston Spa—Field tester and contributor for kindergarten lessons.

Susan Kirby-Lemon, Librarian at Skano Elementary School, contributed her lessons on cause and effect and Mythbusters. Brain Tracker developed from "Inquiry Tracker" provided by Susan and Liz Bailey.

Okte Elementary School Students and Radez Elementary School who contributed their testimony.

Maria Weeks, Librarian, Schuylerville Elementary School, Schuylerville, NY—Field tester and contributor.

Katrina Williams, elementary librarian, Greenwich, NY—Field tester and contributor.

Agnes Zeller, grade 4 teacher at Bern Knox Westerlo Elementary School, who shared her forest field trip with scientific thinkers and lesson on Deciduous and Coniferous Forests.

# INTRODUCTION: WHY THINKING?

## THINK TANKS, PROBLEMS, AND CREATIVITY . . . A BEAUTIFUL MIND

*A crisis arose in our household years ago, when a March thaw combined with heavy rain, flooded our basement. As buoyant objects began to float about, and water rose to above the ankles, a panic beset the dad of the house, as he locked in on rising water with no apparent way to stop it or get rid of it. Evacuation and selling the wrecked house for peanuts were the best ideas he could come up with.*

*Enter six-year-old David, deflecting parental frenzy: Attempting to initiate a quiet in the storm, a time to think and consider, he stated the following: "Now wait a minute. Just let me think. I will figure something out. I am a problem solver."*

Indeed, in Grade 1, his teacher had framed her year with problem solving and transparent thinking. Her thinkers internalized the skills. Later *Dave-the-Thinker* invented a number of innovative devices to solve family problems, such as a dog foot washer to prevent dirty dog tracks on the kitchen floor.

Floods notwithstanding, David represents his species. He is, as we all are, a problem solver. Equipped with a short-term memory that has a finite capacity, our complex brains are wired to solve problems as a key to survival. We can access and process data, employ it to set learning goals, and create solutions. Our brains consolidate and diffuse bits and pieces into meaningful concepts. They predict with a discipline specific knowledge base, categorized to quickly fit circumstances that arise.

Inquiry learning and project-based learning are powerful essentially because they are brain-based. Some correlations between inquiry and brain-based learning include:

- Building of background knowledge, big ideas, and vocabulary of the discipline
- Tapping of prior knowledge and prior attitude
- Building strong real-world scenarios
- Making personal choices
- Investigating experientially
- Using multiple resources in many formats
- Coaching and feedback at point of need
- Making emotional connections
- Interacting socially
- Constructing meaning
- Focusing on connections

- Ongoing questioning
- Reflecting on metacognition
- Seeking and evaluating information
- Forging patterns, relationships and building big ideas
- Wondering and curiosity that engages the learner

Recent decades have given birth to cognitive science, introducing educators to how the brain works. Applying brain science to learning allows us to improve teaching and student performance. Many books have been written around *brain science* and this book does not intend to compete with that vast body of research. However, that same research has led us to the positions we espouse in this book as applied to our work educating students.

Inquiry is the framework for the deep brain learning experiences in this book. Fostering deep thinking and the development of an *expert mind* is the central focus of this book. The assumption that classrooms and schools can be think tanks will be demonstrated in the sample lessons. Truly, if they are not think tanks, classrooms will diminish their potential to implement the Common Core Learning Standards. They diminish their potential to move beyond rote, and fact-soaked brains with no possibility for content mastery.

Progression for the novice brain to the expert brain is the heart of the matter for college and career readiness. Progression from novice to expert brain is our responsibility and our charge. It is essential to achievement and our economic future. We are educating the next generation that will run the world. This mission is not only critical, it is imperative.

Universities have the impression that K-12 educators require only rote and recall from their students. This advice to professors from Columbia University is incriminating:

> Students must recognize the limitations of their current skills, knowledge, and perspectives. They must realize that approaches rewarded in high school—such as rote memorization, the mechanical use of formulas, or the parroting back ideas from a textbook—are no longer sufficient in college, where we value originality, high-level analytical skills, and facility in writing.
> [http://www.columbia.edu/cu/tat/pdfs/Transformational%20Teaching.pdf]

This book is an amalgamation of brain research. Our bibliography represents years of reading, learning, embracing, and implementing brain-based educational recommendations. We did not do the research, but we assimilated this and put it into practice. It's time to take thinking seriously and equip the leaders of tomorrow to change our world!

# CHAPTER 1

# THINKING AND THE CULTURE
# OF YOUR SCHOOL

The pure, original think-tank phenomenon inspired this book. Although the prototype is not a perfect match for the culture of a school, the Common Core does encourage a culture of collaboration true to the think-tank model. Think tanks are essentially defined by: expertise, collaboration, research, and the focus on a *problem*. This can easily be mirrored in a library, classroom, or a school.

Pinterest is populated with think-tank classroom ideas. Prepackaged think-tank bulletin board die cuts, student awards, and stickers are for sale on Google. Also, many project-based and inquiry-driven classrooms feature think-tank spaces, think-tank resources, and instructional goals related to thinking.

A virtual tour of think-tank culture in schools abounds in colorful manipulatives, activities, and brain teasers. A think-tank tour would include student directed investigations, collaborative learning ventures, real-world experiences, and problem solving. Think-tank references align into three tiers:

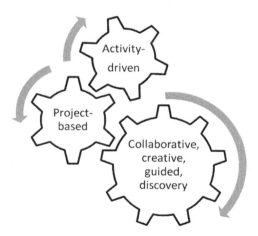

Tier three genuinely encompasses the best thinking, as well as collaborative, creative, and problem-centered student work. This requires a supportive learning environment where students are safe to question, investigate, brainstorm and refine their discoveries based upon information, evidence, and thought. At this level, knowledge of the discipline and its language is the starting point.

Think tanks are real-world. Generating and advocating for public policy is often done in a think-tank model. Government and corporate interests support think tanks to address problems, issues, and

| Does this foster college & career readiness? | Does this work for a think-tank model? | Objectives Aligned with the Common Core and College and Career Readiness |
|:---:|:---:|---|
| ✓ | ✓ | *Research to deepen understanding* |
| ✓ | ✓ | Communication of original and unique ideas |
| ✓ | ✓ | Speaking and listening in a climate of critical engagement |
| ✓ | ✓ | Synthesizing data and texts |
| ✓ | ✓ | Shaping useful habits of mind, thinking dispositions, and thinking skills |
| ✓ | ✓ | Connecting to problems and issues in the real-world |

opportunities. Scientific research often occurs in a think-tank setting. NASA solved the problems with *Apollo 13* in a frenzied, collaborative, and problem-based crisis, and the mission was saved by expert thinking. The economy and the well-being of millions are pushed forward daily by think tanks in informal, low-profile settings.

Some aspects of the Common Core dispose classrooms and teachers to use a think-tank approach to problems and issues. Using knowledge for a meaningful purpose requires higher-level thought. Primary source texts, background knowledge, and key concepts generate topics to be explored, uncovered, and investigated.

Think-tank classrooms and think-tank schools transform learning with purpose, energy, and motivation. Learners can experience genuine flow in their collaborative work, moving beyond the clock and irrelevant tasking. Learners can enjoy awareness of cognition and successful solutions. New ideas, pride in rigorous work, and purposeful analysis reward those in think-tank classrooms and think-tank schools.

# CHAPTER 2

# 22 STRATEGIC IDEAS FOR TURNING YOUR LIBRARY INTO A THINK TANK TODAY

Consider the following suggestions as brain basics. You can optimize instruction and learning by using these brain strategies in your library or classroom. If you weave these in routinely, there will be a significant difference in the dynamics of your library. A learner-centered environment generates and stimulates thinking. Using these multipurpose *think-tank tools* often result in innovative ideas to take thinking to a new level. Conscious use of these tools can become habitual and natural. Skill increases with use. Each strategy aligns with research on how the brain learns and what works optimally for active learners.

*It is the supreme art of the teacher to awaken joy in creative expression and knowledge.*

Albert Einstein

1. **Elicit emotion**

    When emotion is in play, the brain focuses better and remembers what is learned. Carefully pay attention to emotion—a much underestimated component of learning. Motivation, purpose, and personal connections all thrive when emotion is tapped. Emotion can transform a disaffected learner and generate enthusiasm in a student who doesn't care. Music, film, stories, pictures, and experience help trigger an emotional response.

2. **Connect, connect, connect**

    Short-term memory has a finite capacity. The brain can move many facts into long-term memory by chunking details under broad categories. Charting, concept mapping, mind mapping, and Web 2.0 tools that visualize connections help to discern relationships among discrete items. Connecting elements of text to experience, or people to ideas, doubles the likelihood of getting the brain to pay attention and file the idea into memory. Otherwise, it will be treated like background noise. Consciously connect new content to prior knowledge. Recycling ideas, essential questions, and concepts strengthens neural pathways. Conventional wisdom says: *neurons that fire together wire together.*

3. **Talk, socialize, interact, and collaborate**

    The human brain is hardwired for social interaction. Learning in a solitary and silent mode is not optimal for memory. Learning in a socially interactive setting is characterized by sharing, feedback, discussion, critical engagement, or conversation. This "turns on the lights" for the brain, as Ross Todd posits. The quality of decisions made with peer involvement surpasses those generated solo.

Knowledge products produced by teams collaboratively which merge diverse talents and strengths are stronger than those created by one mind.

4. **Be quiet**

   After an interval of multitasking or diverse learning experiences, the brain has a tough job to accomplish. To process important new ideas, the brain needs to consolidate what it has in temporary holding. This complex activity requires a quiet, inactive time such as a break, or even sleep. Taking multiple breaks at intervals from sustained activity gives the brain its quiet time to go to work consolidating. Intense, sunrise to sundown exposure to media, relentless entertainment, and minute-to-minute texting defeats the brain's efforts. Sleep is the last resort.

5. **Think aloud**

   Model your expert brain in action, verbalizing what you are thinking. Call attention to the thinking process when solving problems or tackling tough text, when making an important decision or weighing pros and cons. Place a real or virtual sign over your doorway: Thinking in progress. Activate your brain. This is often referred to as metacognitive modeling.

6. **Challenge with rigor**

   It is counterintuitive, but the brain responds to rigorous content with equally rigorous thinking. Nature seeks the easy path, and brains do too. Quick decisions and a surface grasp of concepts appeals to the line of least resistance in the brain. Many learners think they know when they are merely familiar with a concept. This can be a barrier to really knowing content. Low-level thought is not likely to get neurons firing or connecting. Rigorous and meaningful work actually leads to deep understanding, when the brain grapples with understanding, reasoning, questioning, and evaluating. Dilemmas are valuable and worth a thousand flat, airless facts.

7. **Engage the power of reflection and metacognition**

   Self-assessment, metacognitive thinking, and the habit of evaluating one's own progress all boost learning and the quality of products. Stopping to consider what is accomplished against a model, a rubric, or a reflection with a peer helps the learner to confront problems and use feedback to improve performance. A fast-track task that starts like a footrace, whisks through the essentials, and lands in the done pile with a thud can be completed without thinking. Unfortunately the thinking makes the learning happen. Thinking is the true essential.

8. **Question**

   Questions are catalysts of thinking. Thinking is the catalyst for learning. Learning is ultimately not based in answers, but in questions. Questions can spark curiosity, probe deeper reasons, clarify foggy notions, or challenge assumptions. Questions redirect the flow of ideas back to the learner. They uproot misconceptions and insist on better evidence. Questions scaffold understanding from *what* to *how* and *why*. Questioning is at the heart of the Common Core because of their connection to thinking.

9. **Answer questions with questions**

   Every librarian has heard their share of "stupid questions" despite the old claim that there is no such thing. We beg to differ. We can answer those questions with another question to help metacognitively model the path of deductive reasoning. When you hear a stupid question such as, "Do you have any good books?" you can respond with the better mode, "Well, how do you define "good," Johnny?

10. **Solve authentic problems**

    The human brain is a problem-solving brain. Failing to use the power of authentic problem-solving in teaching and learning is like pushing a high-powered sports car up a hill. So much content easily converts into a problem-based framework. It is like turning on the ignition and roaring down a thinking highway. The beauty of problems is that they have no immediate answers. Brains need to analyze, evaluate, synthesize, and conclude to work with them. That level of thinking assures transfer and long-term new knowledge.

11. **Be relevant**

    What does this have to do with me? When will I use this again in my life? Why should I care? Students and the brain keep asking those questions. In an efficiency-driven and energy-saving screening process, the brain is constantly dismissing and forgetting the irrelevant. Mental survival does not depend on spelling words or practicing fractions. Hooking a concept area to the learner's own life experience is a bridge prescribed by the Common Core State Standards (CCSS). If learning is relevant to the real-world, and to the learner, the brain processes the incoming information with attention.

12. **Synthesize**

    Bloom's Taxonomy and newer iterations of Depth of Knowledge and Cognitive Rigor stack levels of thinking from rote and recall on the low end, to synthesis at the high-end. The thinking and concluding that discerns connections among related, and even unrelated, is synthesis. Synthesis is the catalyst for transfer. Transfer means that a learner will be able to use new knowledge in other applications. Transfer means cognitive real estate is in place where new and related understanding can grow. Stopping short of synthesis reverts learning back to rote and recall of facts.

13. **Deconstruct and reconstruct**

    Breaking down texts, content, and information into structural and conceptual chunks pulls the brain's focus back to usable big ideas and relationships. Analyzing broad or complex data (information or evidence) into sense-making chunks, increases the likelihood that the brain can wrap itself around new information or knowledge. Looking for patterns, themes, or universal historical frameworks can facilitate mental footholds. Instead of an overwhelming buzz of tiny infoBits, the brain reconstructs pieces into a reasonable and logical web. Building that cognitive frame or schema results in confidence and stamina that sustains thinking.

14. **Inquire and question**

    The inquiry process is an amazing composite of brain-based strategies. Indeed, each step in the inquiry sequence has brain-friendly process in place. **Wonder, investigate, synthesize,** and **express** are innately brain-based steps richly connected to higher-level thought. Turning to a learner centered, knowledge centered, question driven, collaborative, and interactive learning model is the one-stop shopping option too good to pass up. Engaged learners care, personalize connections, think to solve problems and address issues. They communicate and reflect. Inquiry-based learning is ideal to launch thinking.

15. **Manipulate, fool around play**

    Daniel Pink would approve of right-brained strategies to incubate creativity and innovation. Einstein would also agree. Experimentation, hands-on manipulation, experience with robotic software, open-ended engineering dilemmas, and other ways to save the world lend themselves to epiphanies or discoveries or theories. Makerspaces, coding activities, hands-on materials, STEM components, and creative manipulatives deserve our attention and space.

16. **Probe the schema**

    Learners arrive at your door with a preexisting set of notions about almost everything they have encountered in life. Wind happens because trees move. There is no connection between shifts in the distribution of wealth and the decline of labor unions. The way to get more money is to shop and get lots of change. Air quality doesn't have anything to do with me. The case in point is that librarians can open up a conduit to the schema. The strategies to revisit misconceived ideas, and break the robust tethers of wrong thinking, are the portals to understanding the world.

17. **Teach thinking skills**

    Go ahead. Direct instruction of thinking skills with guided practice is the straight path to a goal. Learners need to figure out how to think more expertly. Age appropriate target thinking skills are illustrated in this book. Feedback, stopping to reinforce evidence of thinking, and reflection strengthen the thinking pathways in the brain.

18. **Mix it up, jazz it up!**
Variety is definitely the spice of life, and the spice of thinking. The brain is always saying to itself: "What's different? What's new?" Nietzsche's famous quote, "Even the gods are bored," is probably true enough. Learners grind down to glassy-eyed sloggers when the input is a droning remake of yesterday's course. This is not complicated. Take a visual approach today, the auditory approach tomorrow. Dance, sing, and sculpt the way they do in Waldorf Schools. Get kids to generate captions and cartoons. Make iMovies. Recreate a living historical event on the Underground Railroad. Use the whiteboard today, the Library of Congress photo archive tomorrow. Speak, listen, read aloud. Interview. Take digital pictures. Write a collaborative poem, a dialog. Virtually visit the poles or the bottom of the sea. Skype. Blog. Publish or take a trip. The possibilities are endless.

19. **Inquire: Use Socratic dialog**
Ultimately evidence of understanding needs to be elicited. Demonstrate that safe little packaged answers are often going to be poked, and expanded. Ask, *What do you mean?* Create a culture of critical engagement. Use Socratic questioning to convince learners that inch deep will not cut it. *Can you say that in another way? Why would you assume that? Have you experienced that yourself? What evidence exists that this is true? Where did you find that information? Is that a reliable source?* Make that skeptical posture a regular part of your repertoire.

20. **Add choices and voices**
The importance of choice and personal voice cannot be overstated. Once again turning the tables and making the learner the center of the dynamic lights up the brain like a 4$^{th}$ of July picnic. Communicating original conclusions, making decisions, solving problems, and addressing meaningful issues get the gears turning. The learner is invested. Motivation kicks in. Ownership changes everything. Personal agency, according to Ross Todd, is the result of this shift. The learner can say with confidence: "I care. I count. I can."

21. **Insure safety and reduce stress**
When the brain is stressed, it reverts to a flight or fight mode that is not amenable to learning or thinking. Still in touch with survival instincts, the brain is distracted by fear, uncertainty, threats, worry, or suffering. Making the library a safe learning environment is a fundamental and essential predisposition to thinking and learning. Comfort, respect, stimulation, opportunity, community, success, and support can be built in everyday for everyone.

22. **Generate and create then celebrate!**
Research on writing, reading, and thinking recommends the principle that all learners need to be productive. Publishing, posting, sharing, displaying, and creating would show up in an MRI of the brain like the lights of Times Square. A celebratory moment rejuvenates, bonds, and prompts the all-important reflection. Work that does not matter finds its way into trash cans or into high school lockers for cleanout day. What has been meaningfully accomplished, as a generative and collaborative learner, will brighten the light of the mind indefinitely.

# CHAPTER 3

# THINK-TANK LIBRARIES AND INQUIRY

When is a question the answer?
When is solving a problem the perfect way to engage learners?
When is rigorous and challenging work the best kind?
When does collaboration and communication super-charge learners?
When is brain-based learning firing and wiring neurons?

The answer is, *When the library is a think tank!*

Learning theory confirmed by neuroscientists has infused the Common Core, the new C3 Framework for Social Studies, and the Next Generation Science Standards. The common thread, which is more like a rope binding these together, is Inquiry learning. The rationale for this is straightforward: it works. Learners reach deep and lasting understanding of their world through Inquiry.

Can school librarians see themselves in these standards? Are school librarians optimizing the power of brain-based learning? Are they innovating to be ready for critical thinking and information literacy so

evident in these standards? This is a time of incredible opportunity. School librarians need to engage with the C3 Framework and its inquiry-bones: *developing questions, planning inquiries, evaluating sources, using evidence, and communicating conclusions and taking informed action*. School librarians need to celebrate Inquiry in the Next Generation Science standards. They need to engage with their problem solving approach and the embedded ELA standards that lead to writing, research using multiple sources, arguments, and evidence-based claims.

Our 2014 book *Rx for the Common Core: A Toolkit for Implementing Inquiry Learning*, explicitly defines the power of Inquiry to engage and empower learners. Real-world guidance for teachers and librarians evolved from over six years of embedded coaching in real schools.

Inquiry has deep roots in brain research. Understanding how kids learn is the basis for effective pedagogy. Many instructional practices ignore brain research, and get poor results. Passive learners who listen-to-learn retain very little of what they hear—perhaps as little as 5 percent after 2 weeks. Active learners engaged in inquiry achieve long-term understanding of content. Essential questions and big ideas drive deep understanding and the construction of meaning. Learning characterized by background building, attention to prior knowledge, questioning, investigation, original conclusions, synthesis, and communication, results in lasting and flexible new knowledge.

One path to growing inquiry is WISE. WISE is an acronym meaning: wonder, investigate, synthesize, and express. The WISE inquiry model provides a script for an inquiry-based learning experience. WISE is compact and diligently grounded in successful curricular models. These models begin with an overarching, essential question aimed at the learning objective. This model embraces higher-level thinking.

Children in the Okte Elementary School in Clifton Park, New York have shared their voices in defining WISE, the inquiry model they use in pursuing their research investigations:

## Essential Questions

"Behind all of our amazing work, we have questions to answers and we call them Essential Questions. These questions are very important to us because they tell us what we are going to do our research on. Our most important Essential Questions for the whole year have been, 'Why does where we live change how we live?' and 'Why is it important to learn about the world?' I have learned information about some countries that made me think different [sic] about them."

## Using a Mentor Text

"By learning about New Zealand first, now I understand what I will be investigating for all of my countries."

## Wonder

"Wonder is the first step in the WISE process for inquiry learning. When we wonder, we are actually beginning our research. We start by thinking of an Essential Question that will help us focus when we research. In our World Scrapbook binder, we have wonder words to help us think. Some of them are how, compare, compare, explain, why, and describe."

## Investigate

"Behind all of our amazing work, we have questions and we call them Essential Questions. These questions are very important to us because they tell us what we are going to do our research on. Our most important Essential Questions for the whole year have been, 'Why does where we live change how we live?' and 'Why is it important to learn about the world?' I have learned information about some countries that made me think different (sic) about them."

## Synthesize

"The 'S' in WISE stands for synthesis. Synthesize means to organize the information we found from our sources. When we are done researching, we take our information and put our notes onto our colored note taking templates. We put all the information in our own words so that we understand."

## Express

" The E in WISE stands for Express. When we express our learning, we show what we have learned in a creative way. Some of the ways we have expressed our learning have been making graphs, Wordless, and art projects. We have also written paragraphs and reported to the others in our U.N. groups."

—Shared with enthusiasm by school librarian Liz Bailey, Grade 5 teacher Karen Robbins, her students, and Principal Lisa Mickle of the Okte Elementary School who have taken the inquiry path.

A complete copy of the WISE inquiry model can be found in *Rx for the Common Core: a Toolkit for Implementing Inquiry Learning* by Mary Ratzer and Paige Jaeger, Libraries Unlimited 2014.

# CHAPTER 4

# THINKING AND THE COMMON CORE

In a broad view, the Common Core is an engine to transform the content and delivery of learning. Tapping research that posits the importance of reading and comprehending complex text, the CCLS acknowledges that critical thinking alone does not improve student performance. However, driving principles of the CCLS align with brain-based learning and the power of thinking. If the CCLS had headlines, they would certainly read:

Higher Standards Focus on Rigor and Relevance
Deep Understanding Linked to Synthesis
Real-World Problem-Solving: Part of Multidisciplinary Approach
Writing Evidence-Based Claims Taps Critical Thinking Skills

Selected evidence from the CCLS solidifies the role of thinking in the standards:

Use their experience and their knowledge of language and logic, as well as culture, to think analytically, address problems creatively, and advocate persuasively.

Delineate a speaker's argument and specific claims, evaluating the soundness of the reasoning and relevance and sufficiency of the evidence, and identifying when irrelevant evidence is introduced.

Present claims and findings, emphasizing salient points in a focused, coherent manner with relevant evidence, sound valid reasoning, and well-chosen details.

Propel conversations by posing and responding to questions that probe reasoning and evidence; ensure a hearing for a full range of positions on a topic or issue; clarify, verify, or challenge ideas and conclusions; and promote divergent and creative perspectives.

Respond thoughtfully to diverse perspectives; synthesize comments, claims, and evidence made on all sides of an issue; resolve contradictions when possible; and determine what additional information or research is required to deepen the investigation or complete the task.

Present information, findings, and supporting evidence, conveying a clear and distinct perspective, such that listeners can follow the line of reasoning, alternative or opposing perspectives are addressed, and the organization, development, substance, and style are appropriate to purpose, audience, and a range of formal and informal tasks.

CCSS English Language Arts Standards.

# Chapter 5

# NOVICE AND EXPERT THINKERS

```
WANTED:
Expert Thinkers
```

That sign hangs on the door of college admissions offices, corporate human resources suites, and small business front doors. College and career readiness (CCR) inherently demands that young learners succeed in their passage from novice to expert thinkers.

The learner who is a thinker-work-in-progress can be spotted in a school library with a simple task assigned by a health teacher:

*Students need to identify and access a single periodical article about the impact of drug use on American teens. A discussion of the articles retrieved would build background knowledge for the class. They would later initiate research on specific problems caused by drug use in high school.*

How is this young man a novice thinker? Let us count the ways:

1. Googler skimmed his choices.
2. Googler picked a short and probably unsuitable piece for the purpose at hand.
3. Googler did not read closely. If he did, it might have made him aware that he was probably going to come up short in the survey of information ahead in the classroom.
4. Novice thinker bypasses the problem with the text, and reads it without a critical perspective.
5. Novice thinker is glad to be done with a task.

Obviously the student lacks deep knowledge of the content area, and also does not care about the content area enough to engage or exert effort. This information pandemic is rampant in our schools with many classroom teachers joining this misinformation mode-of-operation (MO). With one-to-one device initiatives pervasively showing up in classrooms, it is imperative to understand why this model of fact-fetching is rife with problems.

```
┌─────────────────────────────────┐
│  Accessing the Internet instead  │
│  of a database, the novice       │
│  thinker plugs a broad search    │
│  statement into Google.          │
└─────────────────────────────────┘
              ↓
      ┌─────────────────────────┐
      │  The first few hits are  │
      │  scanned.                │
      └─────────────────────────┘
                  ↓
        ┌───────────────────────────────┐
        │  The selection of a very brief │
        │  review of a book about drugs  │
        │  convinces the student that    │
        │  his task is complete.         │
        └───────────────────────────────┘
                      ↓
          ┌──────────────────────────────┐
          │  Printing a postage stamp     │
          │  block of text, a librarian   │
          │  encounters the student and   │
          │  points out the problems with │
          │  the book review as a useful  │
          │  resource.                    │
          └──────────────────────────────┘
                          ↓
            ┌──────────────────────────────┐
            │  Glad to have his work done   │
            │  for the period, the student  │
            │  insists that the article     │
            │  will be fine and proceeds to │
            │  finish his math homework.    │
            └──────────────────────────────┘
```

**What is wrong with simple fact fetching:**

- Isolated details from the book review will do little to construct a meaningful schema
- Facts have a brief shelf life in short-term memory
- Anemic information-fragments, sliced from a website, will not connect to or build concepts or connections
- Whatever prior knowledge or attitude this learner holds will stay in place
- Misconceptions, partial understanding, and wrong ideas live on
- With a fuzzy, partly-constructed mental model of the subject at hand, this learner has no chance to get to the valid and productive questions that will kick start new knowledge
- This learner begins a passage to expertise from a universal base camp of novice actions, judgments, and thinking

Teachers and librarians can be guides for a successful passage to *expert thinking*. **Conscientiously engaging the novice in these steps makes thinking teachable:**

How does this list of strategies uncover the characteristics of expert thinkers? Research by many including De Groot, Glaser, Wineberg, Brandsford, Donovan, Pellegrino, Marzano, Cleary, Zimmerman, Ericsson, and Bruer elucidated many common elements in expert thinking. Experts seem to have what could be called an **Effective Thinking Model**. Teachers and librarians, especially in collaboration, can motivate and guide learners to internalize facets of expert thinking. This book embeds that process in real-world models. When expert thinking is unified into a model, these key elements are consistently present. Note how combining the elements correlate with synthesis.

| | | |
|---|---|---|
| Building background knowledge sufficient to construct meaning | Taking time to build understanding by framing the content in *big ideas* | Framing learning in a problem or essential question |
| Setting goals for learning | Eliciting prior knowledge and attitudes making flawed notions transparent | Engaging the learner in personal connections to the content |
| Establishing relevance with the learner in an active role | Motivating learners to plan in order to solve a problem | Modeling the relationships between details |
| Thinking aloud and modeling higher-level thinking (metacognition) | Using higher-level questions to clarify, deepen, and critique | Leading discussion to capture student thinking |
| Making misconceptions transparent | Interrogating fact, opinion, opposing ideas, and multiple perspectives | Engaging learners in critical analysis |
| Supporting the learner in connecting discreet bits of information with concepts | Modeling the organizational structure of new knowledge through relationships | Emphasizing patterns in new knowledge and their role in meaning |
| Using the big ideas to provide a mental model of the content area | Sustaining learners in close reading as a base for questions | Expecting solid evidence |

*Expert thinkers are:*

| Resourceful & knowledgeable | Strategic & goal-directed | Purposeful & motivated |
|---|---|---|
| • Bring considerable prior knowledge to new learning | • Formulate plans for learning | • Are eager for new learning and are motivated by the mastery of learning itself |
| • Activate that prior knowledge to identify, organize, prioritize, and assimilate new information | • Devise effective strategies and tactics to optimize learning | • Are goal-directed in their learning |
| • Recognize the tools and resources that would help them find, structure, and remember new information | • Organize resources and tools to facilitate learning | • Know how to set challenging learning goals for themselves |
| | • Monitor their progress | • Know how to sustain the effort and resilience that reaching those goals will require |
| | • Recognize their own strengths and weaknesses as learners | |
| • Know how to transform new information into meaningful and useable knowledge | • Abandon plans and strategies that are ineffective | • Monitor and regulate emotional reactions that would be impediments or distractions to their successful learning |

Used with permission: National Center on Universal Design for Learning udlcenter@udlcenter.org

Although every lesson will not display all these elements consciously, the goal is to foster expert thinking in your students so that these characteristics are observable in discussion, investigation, brain storming and concluding. That accomplished—we should feel successful.

| Beginner Thinker: Observer, Recorder | Novice Thinker: Asks questions, wonders why |
|---|---|
| Follows directions to complete | Seeks answers |
| Tasks | Transfers facts |
| Records observations | Challenges thinks |
| Identifies facts | Understands basics, then asks questions |
| Sees no patterns or connections | Transfers meaning—doesn't create new meaning |
| Records as directed | Big ideas still under construction |
| Completes task cooperatively | Clusters related facts under a main idea |
| Meaning is not constructed | Relies on short-term recall |
| May develop vocabulary for future use | Does not fully understand |
| Traps the right answer | |
| **Augmenting Thinker: to build upon—to change** | **Expert Thinker: Innovator** |
| Constructs meaning from text | Uses vocabulary of the discipline knowingly |
| Uses big ideas and conceptual frameworks | Understands relevant concepts deeply |
| Connects prior knowledge | Understands big ideas |
| Connects personal relevance | Plans, strategically develops goals |
| Develops focus questions | Gathers information, answers why |
| Seeks and uses information | Seeks to understand to solve |
| Builds arguments with evidence | Uses the known to solve the unknown |
| Evaluates quality of sources | Creates new meaning |
| Incorporates multiple perspectives | Pursues quality information |
| Understands the problem, issue | continually assessing validity, bias, perspective, purpose, opposing ideas, and gaps |
| Takes and supports a position | |
| Creates new meaning | Organizes new information by concepts |
| Draws conclusions | Self-assesses |
| Synthesizes seemingly unrelated facts into new knowledge | Communicates with a clear point of view |
| Debates, interrogates, self-assesses | Improves |
| Communicates reasonably, logically | Challenges positions and justifies |

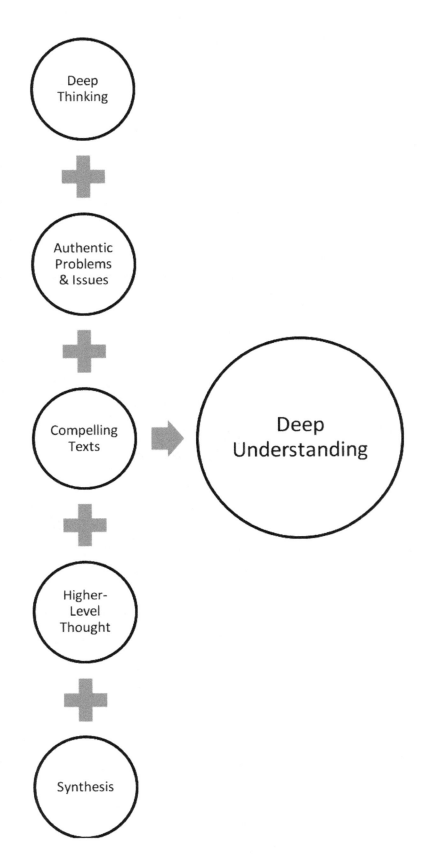

From *Think Tank Library: Brain-Based Learning Plans for New Standards, Grades K–5* by Paige Jaeger and Mary Boyd Ratzer. Santa Barbara, CA: Libraries Unlimited. Copyright © 2015.

# CHAPTER 6

# IF A BRAIN COULD TALK

If a learner's brain could talk to a teacher, what important and strategic points would it try to convey? What reminders would it share? What insights could we gain? The voice of the cognitive scientist would affirm these basics and encourage educators to complete a reality check. Are you optimizing instruction for the brain?

- My short-term memory is limited and does not last very long.
- I am constantly processing a lot of information.
- I am very elastic and making the most synapses from ages 4 to 10.
- I attach new knowledge to old knowledge … somehow making a connection.
- I consolidate patterns so that I can store more related information in chunks. I can classify items into categories to help me store them in the long- term memory.
- The more I already know about something, the easier it is to know more.
- Some input comes from the background around me and some gets more of my attention.
- I tend to monitor and screen out information that is low contrast, because it overloads my circuits.
- I delete things with no value.
- For important information to get my attention it has to have a contrast to the hum of the influx.
- To handle all that information coming in, I have to combine pieces and bits that are related.
- I can quickly filter what is important and not important, once I have experience with information.
- Engage me by spotlighting importance: make it personal, curious, experiential, connected, or real.
- I pay attention to what is unique, emotional, different, or exciting.
- I function exceptionally well with social interaction, and stimulating experiences.
- I use knowledge flexibly and apply it when I understand it better.
- I consolidate facts that are new when I am sleeping or quiet, not when I am playing video games or texting.
- Knowing the vocabulary of new information helps me to learn it.
- Fluency in thinking gets better with knowledge of the subject and its vocabulary.
- I can synthesize and evaluate information.

# CHAPTER 7

# THINKING AND INFORMATION LITERACY

## A WORD GAME

Sort the action words in the text box into two categories: critical thinking and information literacy. If an action fits both categories, place it in both the boxes, and reflect on your results.

> **Analyzing**   **Synthesizing**   **Reflecting**   **Self-assessing**   **Comparing/contrasting**
> **Categorizing information**   **Identifying a problem**   **Solving a problem**   **Evaluating**
> **Inferring**   **Discerning connections**   **Drawing conclusions**   **Supporting a claim**   **Conceptualizing**
> **Arguing with evidence**   **Sorting fact and opinion**   **Questioning**   **Assessing evidence**
> **Exploring multiple perspectives**   **Organizing**   **Communicating**   **Interpreting**

| Thinking | Information Literacy |
|---|---|
|  |  |

This exercise might serve as an object lesson. Every action in the text box belongs in the domain of critical thinking as well as in the domain of information literacy. Mutually reinforcing and coexisting, the two occupy the same space at the same time in an active learner's mind. This has many implications.

Surveying the benchmarks of cognitive development and thinking skills, connections to information literacy and problem solving are not only evident but pervasive. One could argue convincingly that expert thinking is the key to competence, confidence, and success in any number of contexts. Inextricably linked in a powerful alliance, thinking and information literacy join forces in the journey from novice to expert thinker. Arguably, cognitive development, thinking, and information literacy are interdependent. They merge, reinforce, and blend in the cognitive growth of the child and adolescent.

When higher-order thinking skills are enumerated, problem solving, synthesis, inquiry, and metacognition are always identified. The CCSS challenges learners to use critical thinking when closely reading texts, engaging in discussion, writing evidence-based claims, and supporting arguments. All of these depend on information literacy skills that help construct original conclusions with synthesis.

Transforming rather than transferring information requires thinking. Developing focus questions and investigating begins the process. Constructing meaning from multiple texts involves critical thinking. Big ideas evolve from analytical thought, seeking relationships among discrete or even oppositional ideas. Exploration of possible solutions to authentic problems demands a carefully planned inquiry. Diligent assessment of quality of information, validity of conclusions, and relative importance of evidence requires critical thinking, and constitute information literacy.

Comprehension and fact finding, ascertaining the right answer, or searching for the authority with the correct viewpoint do not add up to higher-order thinking. Making the learner responsible for drawing conclusions, setting a goal, or investing in a real-world solution, gears up the level of thinking exponentially. It also gears up the likelihood of long-term understanding. A developing intellect, constructing big ideas, sorting fact from opinion, supporting arguments with evidence, and self-assessing demonstrates aspects of expert thinking and information literacy skills. Using facts and details to support reasoning, reconciling conflicting or incomplete information, incorporating multiple perspectives, a young thinker is information literate.

Theorists who have analyzed thinking processes, including Marzano, Harada, Hester, Crowl, and Facione, agree that thinking and information literacy converge when learners:

- Identify problems, discern issues, seek solutions
- Set a learning goal, plan, and develop questions
- Investigate by evaluating and using information or data
- Verify the reliability, importance, usefulness, and credibility of information or data
- Organize information, synthesize, use evidence to support and argument, and communicate
- Self-assess, reflect

These steps are the information literacy process, and these steps are thinking.

# CHAPTER 8

# THINKING IN ENGLISH LANGUAGE ARTS

*The significant problems we face cannot be solved at the same level of thinking we were at when we created them.*

*Albert Einstein*

A Junior Great Books discussion question for young readers of *Jack and the Beanstalk* could set the stage for an overview of thinking in ELA. "Did Jack solve his problems in the air or on the ground?" The beauty of this question is that it has no apparent or immediate answer. Multiple threads of plot and character need to be woven together to arrive at a conclusion. Analysis and a rudimentary evidence-based claim could be part of the considered response. The brain is engaged in resolving a question with many possible answers.

Learning experiences in ELA can reap the cognitive rewards of higher-level thinking blended with information literacy. Compelling choices of fiction and non-fiction books that launch authentic, collaborative projects, writing, or media production abound. Decision making, planning, engaging, and diverse roles for learners, problem solving and ongoing self-assessment propel ELA brain-based learning with the Common Core. Thinking moves beyond the familiar questions toward essential questions, research questions, and original conclusions. Open-ended questions prompt consideration of multiple perspectives. Young readers who generate questions, build background knowledge, and share perspectives are already in an ELA Think Tank. Reflecting on the visual and literary experience, learners connect to ideas, themes, and inspirations. Extending the story brings satisfaction. ELA is the conduit to deep understanding, empathy, self-knowledge, even outreach to the world.

An elementary example that elucidates this is a learning adventure based-upon *When Marian Sang: The True Recital of Marian Anderson* by Pam Munoz Ryan. This book takes a young learner into a time when racial boundaries stood fast. Despite unprecedented talent as a singer, Marian Anderson could not appear at the great musical venues of her time because of her race. This exquisite picture book portrays a woman of courage and resilience overcoming obstacles, with the help of Eleanor Roosevelt. Long before the civil rights movement, her voice rang out in a rare event on the steps of the Lincoln Memorial. The year was 1939, and a racially mixed audience numbering 75,000 witnessed her amazing talent as a singer. The book lifts the reader's awareness and elicits emotional response. The brain is lighting up.

Marian's boundaries and ways she overcame her challenges would lead to further non-fiction reading for a purpose. Connecting to other talented Americans who overcame boundaries of any kind opens up a gate to authentic research. Learners could further investigate and draw conclusions about Jackie Robinson, Tuskegee Airmen, Rosa Parks, Harriet Tubman, *The Day GoGo Went to Vote: South Africa 1994*, or *Richard*

*Wright and the Library Card.* Exploring new American immigrants, Japanese-Americans interned during World War II, or Hispanics assimilating into American communities extends the connections and the depth of understanding.

To some degree traditional instruction in ELA deferred to decoding, fluency, comprehension, vocabulary, plot, characters, theme, chapter tests, three paragraph essays, and the ubiquitous book report. The vignettes offered above are real-world, but also date back decades. Deep thinking, analysis, and synthesis have always characterized ELA literacy. Inquiry with its rich repertoire of thinking skills is no stranger to ELA, and NCTE endorses inquiry in its newest framework for curriculum. (See below)

The National Council of Teachers of English emphasize thinking in their *Framework for 21st Century Curriculum and Assessment.* Some of their literacies include the following:

- Manage, analyze, and synthesize multiple streams of simultaneous information
- Create, critique, analyze, and evaluate multimedia texts
- Independently and collaboratively solve problems as they arise in their work
- Build on another's thinking to gain new understanding
- Use inquiry to ask questions and solve problems
- Critically analyze a variety of information from a variety of sources
- Solve real problems and share results with real audiences
- Make connections between their work and the greater community
- Create new ideas using knowledge gained
- Synthesize information from a variety of sources
- Use information to make decisions

National Council of Teachers of English. *NCTE Framework for 21st Century Curriculum and Assessment.* Copyright 2013 by the national Council of Teachers of English www.ncte.org. Reprinted with permission. http://www.ncte.org/governance/21stcenturyframework. 19 April 2014.

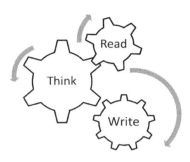

| Low-Level Thinking in ELA | Higher-Level Thinking in ELA |
| --- | --- |
| Remembering | Producing and planning |
| Recalling, retrieving explicit details | Questioning to inquire, questioning across multiple texts |
| Giving examples | Deciding about the theme |
| Categorizing, matching | Focusing on audience and purpose |
| Restating, paraphrasing | Evaluating for bias, relevance, criteria |
| Identifying main ideas and supporting details | Using reason and logic |
| Explaining cause and effect | Validating, verifying, and citing with evidence |
| Predicting | Developing alternatives, multiple perspectives |
| Answering who, what, where, when questions | Concluding what the central message is |
| Making text to self-comparisons | Generating, creating new knowledge |
| Describing | Evaluating claims, organizing, distinguishing relationships |
| Summarizing | Comparing text to text |
| Sorting opinion and fact | Analyzing problems, issues or viewpoints |
| Applying writing conventions | Using syntax and word choice to communicate effectively |
|  | Synthesizing across multiple texts |

# CHAPTER 9

# THINKING AND TEXT DEPENDENT QUESTIONS

Common Core pedagogy shifts include close reading for textual details, for evidence, and for deep meaning. This often happens in the classroom and in the library. However, this generation has an aversion to reading and prefers pictures over print. In order for us to motivate our students to scrutinize and deeply understand the meaning of a primary source document, a book, a passage, an article, or other texts we may have to ask questions that guide their comprehension. These questions are often referred to as text-dependent questions (TDOs).

In our scheduled library time, we can carefully craft our discussions following the recommended pattern below. We start off at the panoramic level asking general and obvious questions—not assuming all students know the basics. From there we can move to concrete fact-type questions which establish the basics of the passage. Once the groundwork has been laid with general and concrete questions, we can move to questions that are challenging. These myopic questions may address a specific CCSS standard such as main idea or inference. From there we can aim for interpretations and deep meaning based upon evidence in the text.

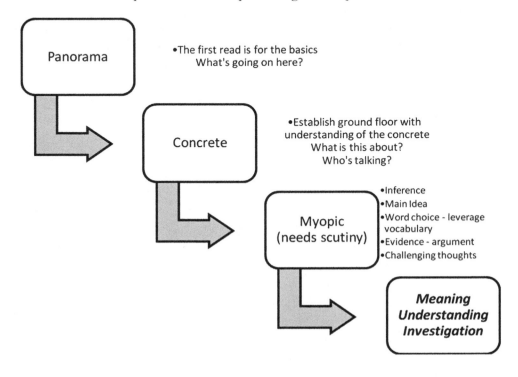

| Brainstorm a TDQ for: | Text-Dependent Questions: |
|---|---|
| Panoramic question | |
| Concrete question—basics | |
| Myopic question needing evidence | If this is about [subject], what is the message? What facts in this text support that main idea? |
| Myopic examination question | How is the word [xxxx] critical to this text's meaning? |
| Summary question for meaning. . . . | |

**Good TDQs will:**

- **Move from concrete to abstract**
- **Cause students to search for meaning**
- **Guide the reader's understanding**
- **Support discovery**
- **Teach a student how to comprehend**
- **Spotlight standards**
- **Should not give away the answer, but cause the student to "discover" it**

Purposeful reading

As you read this book, contemplate your lesson plans and whether you are moving beyond rote and recall in your read alouds, your research endeavors, and learning adventures. Every instructional minute can be carefully viewed as an opportunity to incubate higher-level thought. Text-dependent questions are just the beginning. By nature, a TDQ wants students to carefully read and contemplate the content. A simple read aloud can be transformed with critical TDQs to activate thinking and provide collaborative discussion or debate. In this book you will find a few read alouds turned into brain exercises.

# CHAPTER 10

# THINKING IN SOCIAL STUDIES

*Young people need strong tools for, and methods of, clear and disciplined thinking in order to traverse successfully the worlds of college, career, and civic life.*

*National Council for the Social Studies, College, Career, and Civic Life C3 Framework for Social Studies State Standards, 2013, p. 15.*

The National Council for the Social Studies, the CCSSO, the American Historical Association, and a prestigious collaborative of leading professional groups in the discipline framed a new framework of standards in the social studies. College, Career, and Civic Life C3 Framework for Social Studies State Standards 2013 sets up priorities for teachers that embrace thinking, key conceptual ideas, local choice about how to teach the key ideas in each grade, and a disciplinary structure that reinforces with ever-increasing complexity all important core concepts. Like the CCSS, these frameworks scaffold, extend, and build but hold to the central core. The essence of this document consists of big ideas developed over time, deep understanding, thinking, and decision-making.

Thinking in social studies has a compass. That compass is discipline specific, and it seeks true north in the interpretation of testimony of the past and present to approximate what really happened and why. Truth needs to be winnowed from testimony, records, perspectives, witnesses, biases, half-truths, partial truths, truths that seemed to be true at one point, but are no longer true at all. The compass is guided by disciplined expertise and those rich in content knowledge. Yet new, even declassified documentation continues to present itself. Swings in political attitudes popularize or file away important understandings. Decision making is key to the new framework and must be informed. The challenge for students is to remain skeptical and validating their positions can be daunting.

What does this mean for young learners who are still thinking apprentices? A compilation of guiding principles can be found in the Practices of Social Studies accepted by many educators in the field, and incorporated into New York State's Social Studies Frameworks for example. At each grade level thinking is vertically articulated and consistent. Learners demonstrate these practices with specific and observable performance targets.

Thinking in social studies integrates:

- chronological thinking and causation;
- comparison and contextualization;
- geographic reasoning;
- gathering, using, and interpreting evidence;
- the role of the individual in social and political interpretation.

| Lower-Level Thinking in Social Studies | Higher-Level Thinking in Social Studies |
| --- | --- |
| Describing | Gathering, using, citing evidence |
| Explaining | Distinguishing relevance, usefulness |
| Locating or recalling facts | Solving problems |
| Making lists | Applying concepts, transferring |
| Defining | Distinguishing discreet aspects of issues |
| Collecting, scrapbooking | Evaluating, recognizing misconceptions, validating |
| Comparing | Connecting a concept or theme across time |
| Categorizing, matching | Reasoning chronologically or geographically |
| Explaining cause and effect | Synthesizing from multiple sources |
| Explaining reasons | Interrogating and manipulating multiple perspectives |
| Identifying relationships | Developing arguments |
| Reciting | Using reason, logic, habits of mind |
| Summarizing | Judging by using criteria |
| Giving examples | Planning, producing, creating a new conclusion or perspective |

A number of templates for thinking and cognitive rigor present a fairly unified picture of what lower-level and higher-level thinking look like in social studies. The Depth of Knowledge analysis of Norman L. Webb has been published by the CCSSO, the same organization that sparked the Common Core. *Smarter Balance* assessment guidance documents address cognitive rigor, as do Will Daggett and Karen Hesse. A common distinction of higher-level thinking involves synthesis of multiple information sources, and a learner who is actively engaged with a purpose. Other well recognized matrices have common ground with these ideas regarding low-level and high-level thought in social studies:

# CHAPTER 11

# THINKING IN MATHEMATICS

*Reasoning and sense making are simultaneously the purpose for learning mathematics and the most effective means of learning it. Unless students can reason with and make sense of the mathematics that they are learning, they are likely to ask the age-old question: Why do we need to learn this? They need to see a purpose in studying mathematics beyond the goal of preparing for the next mathematics course or standardized test. Moreover, research shows that students are more likely to retain mathematics that has its foundation in reasoning and sense making than mathematics that is presented as a list of isolated skills.*

National Council of Teachers of Mathematics

## FOCUS IN HIGH SCHOOL MATHEMATICS: REASONING AND SENSE MAKING

The National Council of Teachers of Mathematics considers thinking about mathematics and thinking mathematically as equally important, if difficult to differentiate. Quality mathematical thinking encompasses the attributes of quality thinking in any discipline. Students who can explain math are thinking about math. Reasoning and sense-making are at the heart of thinking in mathematics. Students who answer math questions or solve problems without thinking, reasoning, or sense making do not develop deep understanding. They forget their surface knowledge, and do not retain. Test preparation and drill is soon forgotten, requiring teaching the same skill in the future. Eliciting thinking in math is key to mastery of mathematics.

Mathematical thinking parallels scientific thinking in many ways. Learners identify and restate a problem. Learners analyze the problems and develop a hypothesis about solving them. They consider connections to concepts, other related problems, and evidence. They posit a solution and reflect on it. They test the solution and begin the cycle again.

Math tasks that involve memorization or that reproduce familiar steps require little thinking. The Trends in International Mathematics and Science Study (TIMSS) video analysis of math classrooms in the United States, Germany, and Japan provided evidence of contrasting priorities in the decades before the CCSS. The National Center for Educational Statistics continues to feature access to analysis of TIMSS video archives, as well as the outcomes of TIMSS test results. The TIMSS video documented the role of thinking and conceptual understanding in successful math instruction, and in a way heralded a new vision for the discipline.

Teachers in Japan involved learners in developing solutions to problems, and put maximum value on thinking. Japanese teachers presented a problem, encouraged learners to reflect on solutions, and to suggest solutions. The goal of the teacher was conceptual understanding. Students explained their reasoning, and ultimately knew how the solution evolved. Parts of a lesson were linked to other parts of a lesson,

| Lower-Level Thinking in Math | Higher-Level Thinking in Math |
|---|---|
| Recognizing | Explaining by using concepts |
| Recalling facts | Arguing the validity of a concept |
| Measuring | Explaining a concept |
| Following steps | Applying a concept |
| Reading charts, graphs | Defending an answer when many are possible |
| Charting data | Interpreting a graph or chart |
| Collecting | Selecting graphical information to use |
| Grouping, organizing | Comparing and contrasting |
| Making tables | Analyzing trends, predicting |
| Performing familiar function | Reasoning |
| Practicing a familiar procedure | Using concepts to solve, applying concepts over time |
| Finding a predictable solution | Deciding how to solve with options |
| Observing | Connecting with related problems, solutions, even other disciplines |
| Repeating steps | Synthesizing new understanding |
| Reproducing, copying | Evaluating and criticize analyzing assumptions |
| Substituting | Solving with complex variables |

connecting ideas and concepts. Further, Japanese students applied concepts and invented new solutions, clearly achieving a high-level of thinking.

U.S. classroom video presented evidence of emphasis on practice of skills, stating rather than developing concepts, and using formulas. Lessons were often segmented with many topics addressed in an isolated context. Teachers emphasized homework, reviewed homework, and devoted a large proportion of classroom time to practicing examples of a concept that the teacher covered. Global competition for mathematical competency in the workforce prompted a shift with the CCSS.

The CCSS, with college and career readiness as the greatest priority, frames math standards that stress conceptual understanding, critical thinking, and the ability to apply math to real-world situations. Emphasizing math as the basis for well-founded decisions, the CCSS posits statistics and mathematical concepts as the basis for analysis in everyday life. Planning, evaluating, reflecting, organizing, and observing, as well as other features of expert thinking, are important in mathematical thinking. Rigorous math instruction builds in evidence based argument for concepts and solutions to problems.

The new Common Core Standards in mathematics use a brain-based approach to learning. Each year foundations are built for new learning. A progression of conceptual understanding optimizes the sense of connections for the learner. Grade-by-grade learners extend what they already know, prior knowledge, to develop new knowledge. Math, or any subject, as a long list of formidable topics defies long-term retention and coherence.

Analytical thinking and reasoning empowers learners to draw conclusions from data, compare and contrast ways of solving problems, and generalize. Synthesis caps mathematical thinking, and is the catalyst for innovation, originality, and strategic solutions. Connecting ideas to relevant concepts in order to design models and conduct experiments demonstrates competence in mathematical thinking.

# CHAPTER 12

# THINKING IN SCIENCE

Outside a favorite spot where bear pancakes are served, a pint-sized toddler was stomping around on pieces of broken pavement. Attempting to piece the pavement chunks into the accompanying hole, he did a pretty good job of wedging them together. Brushing off his hands, he said to his mom, "Who broke it? Now tape it."

Not exactly rocket science, but the very young brain was definitely thinking scientifically. Cause and effect, change over time, and problem solving were definitely observable, along with a little engineering. Scientific thinking is hard wired into the developing brain. Five-year-olds seek information, observe, and explore. Like real scientists, learners at an early age are very collaborative, share ideas, give feedback, and wrestle with problems. Children can manipulate and compare objects, describe, draw, and explain. They can use their experience to predict and draw conclusions about current situations, as evidenced when the budding Einstein wanted someone to tape the pavement. Understanding of life science, the environment, earth science, and meteorology grow from early curiosity and wonder.

A study published in 2010, "Science in Early Childhood Classrooms: Content and Process" by Karen Worth, acknowledges the power of early thinking and learning, which was not previously recognized. Worth notes that science is a natural part of early learning, which is sparked by curiosity about the natural world. With this curiosity, children move forward and use inquiry to make sense of their world and develop a host of companion skills in the process.

## AND NOW ON THE HORIZON

School librarians can certainly activate the scientific thinking at any age. A powerful, new platform with meaningful connections for school librarians has arrived on the horizon: *A Framework for K–12 Science Education* and the *Next Generation Science Standards* (NGSS) merge brain-based learning standards with mathematics and ELA standards. True to the CCSS guidelines for scientific literacy, the NGSS frame lessons with *key concepts* and real-world scientific practices. Shifting from content coverage in science, these standards are designed for deep understanding. Here is the really good news: *Evidence-based claims, data driven conclusions, and arguments based on evidence permeate the standards, which culminate in interdisciplinary performance tasks.* The writing and speaking standards address authentic real-world connections. This document has rich potential.

The National Research Council has recently addressed scientific learning and thinking in watershed books: *How Students Learn, Taking Science to School,* and *Education for Life and Work.* Findings in cognitive science characterize their *Framework for K–12 Science Education* and the *Next Generation Science Standards* (NGSS).

It is important to understand that the scientific practices in the *Next Generation Science Standards* (NGSS), as defined by the National Research Council (NRC), include the critical thinking and communication skills that students need for postsecondary success and citizenship in a world fueled by innovations in science and technology. These science practices encompass the habits and skills that scientists and engineers use day in and day out.

Next Generation Science Standards. http://www.nextgenscience.org/frequently-asked-questions. 21 April 2014.

The essence of scientific thinking is the quest for objective and provable truth. Unlike Social Studies where truth is reconstructed through testimony, secondary accounts, and perspectives, science isn't science without fact. Levels of scientific thought reflect knowledge of scientific principle, the evaluation of evidence, and the verification of explanations. Inquiry is a process that integrates scientific thinking to such a degree that the two are indistinguishable in some disciplines. Again, critical thinking and information literacy come together. Inquiry and scientific thinking involve the following:

- Asking questions
- Planning and investigating
- Exploring and accessing information
- Analyzing information
- Evaluating information
- Organizing information
- Constructing meaning from information
- Drawing conclusions substantiated by data or facts, developing hypotheses
- Arguing using evidence
- Communicating information
- Reflecting
- Developing new questions

The scientific method parallels these steps and embodies critical thinking. At every level, scientific thinking leads to objectivity, well-founded decisions, understanding of the invisible and visible world, and analytical habits of mind. Beginning with questions and wonder, scientific thinking and literacy is, in the words of Neil deGrasse Tyson, "the artery through which solutions for tomorrow's problems flow."

| Low-Level Thinking in Science | Higher-Level Thinking in Science |
| --- | --- |
| Recalling a fact or a specific answer | Creating testable questions |
| Asking fact-based questions | Perceiving relationships across texts or disciplines |
| Being aware of accuracy | Organizing and analyzing data |
| Following a procedure, one step | Designing experiments, models |
| Using a familiar formula | Planning an investigation |
| Measuring, defining | Determining relevant and irrelevant information |
| Calculating | Distinguishing bias, incomplete information |
| Gathering data, charting, making a display | Evaluating for validity, precision, logic |
| Selecting useful facts | Self-assessing thinking |
| Categorizing | Interrogating point of view |
| Comparing and contrasting | Conceptualizing critically |
| Representing an idea in a picture | Interpreting |
| Reading a graph | Strategizing |
| Making sense of scientific texts | Drawing original conclusions |
| Writing a summary statement | Synthesizing |
| Observing properties | Solving problems with unpredictable outcomes |
| Recognizing a problem | Reasoning with evidence |

# CHAPTER 13

# INTRODUCTION TO THINK-TANK LESSONS

When planning a lesson, we often weave expectations, learning targets, ideas, and details together in our mind knowing that they "make sense." It is only when we have to write a lesson up for formal observation that we locate the "district approved" lesson plan form and proceed to formally carve the lesson into pieces scrutinizing the worthiness of each part so that we receive a favorable review. That same level of care and concern should now be front and center of all our lessons in order to optimize the use of time for student achievement. Remember—it's all about the kids.

Formal observation has moved beyond pieces fitting together in a delivery to asking, "What can my principal observe, not in my delivery, *but in the students*, to prove that I am an effective teacher?" These students behaviors are sometimes referred to as "dispositions." These dispositions are the evidence of student engagement, and student engagement is the secret to academic success. If the student is not engaged, the student will not learn.

The sample library-classroom lessons that follow are all designed to optimize student engagement. All learning activities are intended to turn rote and recall upside down placing the student at the center of learning. Flip your lessons. Use these models to learn how students can do the learning, digging, investigating, brainstorming, and more. As you read these lessons, you will find repetitive pieces woven together to insure your students are challenged to move to the top of Blooms Taxonomy and beyond. These lessons are intended to embrace multiple CCSS shifts into each lesson thus exemplifying how the librarian can move beyond a simple read aloud to weaving together multiple goals of the CCSS to and become vital member of the instructional team.

The Common Core demands an integrated model of literacy throughout our instruction. Consider this quote from the standards:

*Although the Standards are divided into Reading, Writing, Speaking and Listening, and Language strands for conceptual clarity, the processes of communication are closely connected, as reflected throughout.*

With that in mind, the lessons that follow have been crafted to weave together reading, writing, speaking, and listening. These lessons demand rigor and relevance; embrace multiple instructional shifts; and optimize library instructional time. Our lessons examined critical components such as the rigor of materials, *to* the integration of innovative assessment examples.

# CHAPTER 14

# DEVELOPMENTAL SPOTLIGHT ON THINKING

## THE PRIMARY GRADES: KINDERGARTEN THROUGH FIRST GRADE

Learners who are entering school have developed thinking skills. Integrating these skills into learning experiences, and developing the level of the skills are keys to future performance and confidence. The brain-conscious teacher will carefully craft lessons to embrace skills as well as thought.

**Primary Learner**
- Understands cause and effect
- Examines, manipulates, and experiments
- Explores by asking questions
- Learns by experience
- Perceives the reason for an event
- Compares and contrasts, evaluates
- Explains, uses reason
- Communicates observations
- Builds knowledge
- Discusses problems

**Typical Brain**
- Answers questions with facts: who, what, where, when
- Categorizes
- Is growing optimally and rapidly
- Compares, contrasts, evaluates
- Wonders why
- Explains based upon limited understanding
- Lacks understanding of time
- Blends reality with fantasy

**What Works**
- Charting and collecting information
- Discussing
- Sharing
- Categorizing
- Patterning
- Observing
- Predicting
- Determining cause and effect

## SPOTLIGHT ON THINKING—GRADE 2

Second graders have made giant steps in their cognitive development worthy of spotlighting here. They exhibit confidence in what they can do and what they know. Confident and often aware of other's feelings, they use their emerging skills and social intelligence. Seconds grade thinkers:

- Expands vocabulary by reading and talking, adding to fluency
- Listen and retain information that is heard
- Listen actively and participate in groups
- Understand information that is read in multiple texts
- Follows multiple step directions
- Focus on tasks longer
- Develop individual learning style
- Have a need to know and ask questions
- Plan with multiple steps
- Ask questions to understand more clearly or deeply
- Answer questions with multiple information sources
- Solve problems with creative and complex solutions
- Use logic to solve problems
- Identify and solve problems using the views of others
- Connect concepts to experience
- Locate facts and information
- Compares and contrasts objects
- Sequence events in a basic order, write narratives that recount actions
- Support opinions with reasons
- Make decisions with confidence
- Predict and then test their ideas
- Observe the world and make predictions based on what is observed
- Discuss thinking when solving math problems
- Ascribe characteristics to what is observed
- Reflects on thinking

Take time to assess your lessons to insure you are tapping into the correct cognitive development of the emerging reader. Instructional time is too valuable to waste by not challenging our students. Use a highlighter and highlight items on the list above to give yourself credit for what you've embraced, as well as identify what you can target. Be sure to note cognitive targets in your educational portfolio or identify these in your observations.

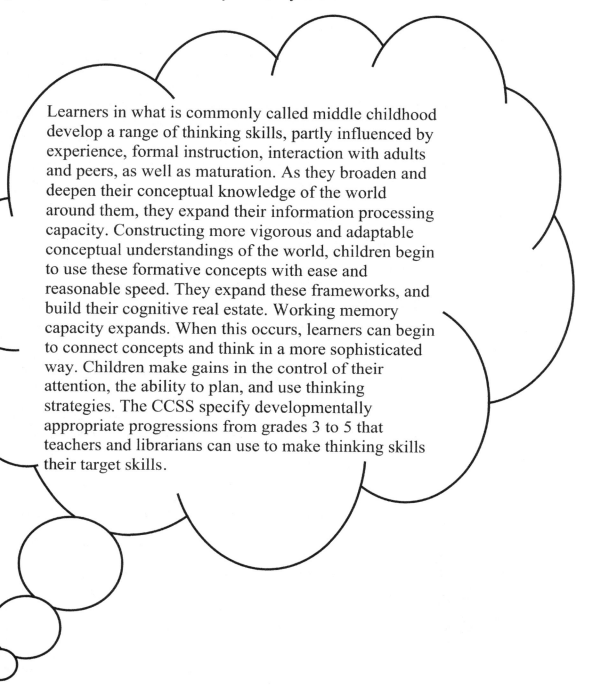

Learners in what is commonly called middle childhood develop a range of thinking skills, partly influenced by experience, formal instruction, interaction with adults and peers, as well as maturation. As they broaden and deepen their conceptual knowledge of the world around them, they expand their information processing capacity. Constructing more vigorous and adaptable conceptual understandings of the world, children begin to use these formative concepts with ease and reasonable speed. They expand these frameworks, and build their cognitive real estate. Working memory capacity expands. When this occurs, learners can begin to connect concepts and think in a more sophisticated way. Children make gains in the control of their attention, the ability to plan, and use thinking strategies. The CCSS specify developmentally appropriate progressions from grades 3 to 5 that teachers and librarians can use to make thinking skills their target skills.

**Later Elementary Learner**
- Understands cause and effect, change over time, point of view
- Reasons based on facts and observations, evidence
- Develops self-aware about thinking and learning
- Connects related ideas with conceptual awareness
- Expands knowledge
- Creates a platform for meaning
- Chunks information beyond concrete categories
- Grows with confidence, metacognition becomes more sophisticated
- Thinks strategically and control of thinking grows
- Stores new knowledge easier with more "prior knowledge"

**Typical Brain**
- Metacognition becomes more sophisticated and productive since brain is rapidly growing
- Focus is increasingly key to performance in complex tasks, writing, and communicating
- Planning and goal setting evolve from amateur to apprentice
- Multiple causes and multiple effects can be understood and manipulated
- Multiple perspectives can be identified
- Long-term and effects can be distinguished
- Change over time can be discerned and represented
- Relationships among patterns and processes are recognized
- Different forms of evidence are analyzed to construct meaning
- Inference begins and can be fostered by looking at relationships
- Expanding and structured networks in the brain facilitate retention of new knowledge
- Organization of mental tasks becomes faster and more extensive
- Memory strategies begin to support new learning

**What Works:**
- Chunking information—connecting information—concept mapping expands awareness and tracks learning
- Linking ideas within and across categories employs language that makes distinctions support for opinions
- Reasoning based on facts requires evidence. Why?
- Using tools for self-assessment that boost progress and performance
- Moving questions from facts to HOW, WHY, SHOULD, WHAT IF
- Start requiring multiple perspectives to enhance understanding
- Integrating information from sources is increasingly based on evaluation of that information
- Different forms of evidence are analyzed and used to construct meaning
- Inference requires analysis of point of view, authorship, and purpose
- Integrating information from sources is increasingly based on evaluation of that information
- Ordering ideas increasingly demands logic, reflection, and analysis
- Drawing conclusions and genuine synthesis is easier

# CHAPTER 15

# PRIMARY K–2 LIBRARY AND CLASSROOM LESSONS

**Bugs Are Beautiful**                                    **Kindergarten 1–2 lessons**

## WHAT'S THE BIG IDEA?

The Next Generation Science Standards would like us to incubate scientific thinking in our youngest learners. This lesson gives students the opportunity to think critically, making connections. Even the youngest learners enjoy asking questions, and this lesson lends the opportunity to ask many questions and discover many answers. Starting with colorful engaging photos, picture books of insects, bugs, and other creatures, the teacher-librarian should metacognitively model some deep observations of color, art, math, and science within the insect world. Butterflies are easily observed as having wings in the shape of triangles, two antennas, and four wing segments.

This metacognitive model could then be done with the class as a whole picking a photo of another interesting bug. A simple Symbaloo.com Web page could be used with a whiteboard. Explanation perhaps as a sidebar of Symbaloo, how to use, where to find, and so on, for the readers who do not know.

Symbaloo is a great free online tool. At Symblaoo, you can line up URL hyperlinks that easily open a Web page when clicked. This is a simple way to prechoose great photos. In fact, you could have a "tab" for different insects, colors, or the focus of your choice.

If you examine the previous page *Introduction to the Primary Brain*, you will see that this lesson includes investigation, wonder, blending, categorizing, recognizing patterns, discussion, and more. This models a simple scientific mindset. This introduces Science Technology Engineering and Mathematics STEM at the early stages. Students will think, compare, contrast, connect, conclude, reason, and more. This lesson leaves room for differentiation for students, for example, who may recognize "symmetry" even though that isn't part of your curriculum.

| Lesson | Bugs Are Beautiful |
|---|---|
| **Learning Targets** | Students investigate and observe for details.<br>Students make connections among science, math, and art.<br>Learners read closely for details.<br>Learners connect details to synthesize. |
| **Essential Questions:**<br><br><br><br>**Guiding Questions:** | How are bugs, art, and math similar?<br>Which bug should win the artistic award? Why?<br>What math do you see in bugs?<br>What color and art do you connect with bugs?<br>How does a bug display math and art?<br>How does close observation help us see differently?<br>How do bugs display artistic beauty?<br>Do we look at things differently, if we "examine" them?<br>Can we find similarities in two seemingly different items? |
| **Text** | *Insect Bodies* by Bobbie Kalman.<br>Any other nonfiction books on bugs, insects, shapes with related colorful engaging texts.<br>Pictures books for this lesson should have pictures more prominent than text.<br>Shapes cutout of construction paper, or plastic manipulatives of shapes.<br>Magazines such as *Ranger Rick*, *National Geographic for Kids* or other texts heavy in colorful photos will serve the purpose of this lesson.<br>Possible use of websites in a Symbaloo.com line-up if your classroom or library includes a Smartboard. |
| **Power words** | Bug, insect, thorax, antenna, wings, legs, pinchers, piercers.<br>Circle, square, rectangle, triangle, trapezoid, diamond, and any other shape encountered. |
| **Vocabulary of library discipline** | Facts, examine, record, listen, closely read, synthesize, observe, compare. |
| **Science Standards** | Next Generation Science Standards ask kindergarten students to be "gathering, describing and using data between the natural and designed worlds." Students should be making connections. This simple lesson is an endeavor to activate thinking in this way.<br>Copyright 2013 Achieve, Inc. All rights reserved |
| **CCSS Objectives Observable in Students** | Participate in collaborative conversations with diverse partners about *kindergarten topics and text*. Cite details about conclusions drawn. With prompting and support, ask and answer questions about key details |

| CCSS Goals | | | | | | |
|---|---|---|---|---|---|---|
| **CCSS<br>Goals** | x | Vocabulary use | x | Answer real-world questions | x | Discuss, interpret, explain |
| | x | Nonfiction use | x | Research | x | Collaboration |
| | x | Close reading | x | Build and present knowledge | x | Rigor |
| | x | Examine | x | Draw conclusions based on evidence | x | Relevance |

| | |
|---|---|
| **Rigor** | This lesson turns young minds into investigative scientists asking students to record details and draw conclusions. With guidance and support, learners will observe similarities and differences. |
| **Relevance** | Children are natural explorers. This lesson gives children a chance to make connections and draw conclusions. Personal voice and sharing observations fosters scientific thinking in a young child. By asking students to connect observed details, students demonstrate their knowledge of math and science within the context.<br>A student's natural world includes bugs and color. Appreciation for a greater understanding of color, art, and math should result from this close examination activity.<br>When learners are generating questions they are at the center of the learning experience. |
| **Listener and the task** | • Students examine books and make observations on color, shape, art, and math.<br>• Students analyze and list their observations.<br>• Students record shapes observed.<br>• Students collaboratively discuss colors.<br>• Students share their observation with their class.<br>• Students produce and present correlations of art and math with insect pictures.<br>• Students speak and respond to questions in the first person as interviewed, during an Open House Night, or lunch hour.<br>• Students speak and respond to questions posing as scientists, using scientific vocabulary.<br>• Students record and find and chart important facts.<br>• Working with an art teacher, create an artistic rendition with color, shapes and observations on an insect of their choice.<br>• Art connections and replications are displayed and explained. |
| **Assessment** | Formative assessment can be captured by asking why are bugs like art and science?<br>What math do you see in bugs?<br>How can you describe and draw a bug using numbers and shapes?<br>Summative assessment includes the same questions which now have answers. Open House Night presentations works easily to document success. |
| **Think Tank Spotlight** | This lesson engages the student to explore by asking questions.<br>Students will learn by experience and observation.<br>Students will synthesize what they know about art and science and math. Different subjects are woven together in the real-world.<br>Students will strengthen their understanding of relationships.<br>Students will be required to explain, use reasoning, and communicate to express their knowledge. |

| **Bloom's Barometer** | Remembering | Understanding | Applying | Analyzing | Evaluating | Creating |
|---|---|---|---|---|---|---|
| | x | x | x | x | x | x |

# I Need You, You Need Me!                    Kindergarten, 1–2 lessons

## WHAT'S THE BIG IDEA?

This kindergarten lesson spotlights how you can use an old book with a timeless meaning. Eric Carle's books are timeless and his *House for Hermit Crab* lends us the opportunity to activate thinking, embrace shifts in the new standards.

If the early learner's brain can: collect information, engage in discussion, share, observe, predict, and identify cause and effect, then this book gives us a great opportunity to use all these metacognitive strategies. Even though students cannot write to document all their thinking, we can use discussion to both assess learning and insure all students get an ample opportunity to think and share.

Please note that the Essential and Guiding Questions are scaffolded for each of the cognitive strategies. An experienced teacher may want to compare this lesson to the way this Carle book may have been used in the past, in order to note the focus on thinking over content.

As new standards ask us to concentrate on vocabulary, building knowledge, and backing up our claims with evidence, we can do that with this book. Eric Carle purposely chooses to embed valuable vocabulary—both academic as well as scientific—in this book. Student's use of vocabulary is an easy way to assess success. In knowledge products, we expect students to embrace the new vocabulary as proof of their learning.

As students create knowledge poster products of their chosen "sea community member," they will synthesize strengths of that creature and the contribution they make to the community.

This lesson based upon a suggestion by a certified K-2 teacher, Stacie Hawkins Jaeger, incubates expert thinkers at the earliest stages of formal education. Einstein would be happy.

| Lesson: | I need you. You need me. Kindergarten |
|---|---|
| Learning Targets: | Students listen and observe for details.<br>Students make connections between needs, wants, and service.<br>Learners connect details to synthesize how strengths and characteristics foster ways to help others. |
| Essential Questions: | How are we mutually interdependent?<br>How do animals depend on each other?<br>How do sea creatures (animals) use their strengths and their physical characteristics to survive and solve problems?<br>How does valuable vocabulary help to describe things?<br>When a valuable vocabulary word is used, how does that enhance meaning? |
| Guiding Questions: | How can/do we help each other? (Discuss, share, recognize.)<br>How can we help meet the needs of our family, friends, or neighborhood? (predict, share, discuss, recognize)<br>How are we like the hermit crab?<br>How have people helped us? (cause and effect)<br>How did the hermit friends help him? (snails helped clean house, the sea urchins helped protect, and the glowfish provided light)<br>Ask students, in what ways are they like [hermit crabs]?<br>What valuable vocabulary words did Eric Carle use to describe [coral]?<br>How does the word [whisper] help paint a better picture? Why?<br>What additional questions might you have about animals, helping, needs, or homes? |

| | |
|---|---|
| | Can you think of other animals that might help each other? (Cats carry their young in the mouth; kangaroos carry their young; mothers feed children.) |
| **Text** | *A House for Hermit Crab* by Eric Carle |
| **Power words** | Academic vocabulary: Abdomen, threaten, withdraw, snug, frightened, swayed, dependent<br>Science vocabulary: anemone, characteristics, coral, habitat, hermit crab, house, plankton, pollution, shell, skeleton, snail, starfish |
| **Vocabulary of library discipline** | Facts, examine, record, listen, closely read, synthesize, cause and effect |
| **Science Standards** | Next Generation Science Standards ask kindergarten students to be "gathering, describing and using data between the natural and designed worlds." Students should be making connections. This simple lesson is an endeavor to activate thinking as scientists, noting needs, cause and effect relationships and more<br>Copyright 2013 Achieve, Inc. All rights reserved |
| **CCSS Objectives Observable in Students** | Participate in collaborative conversations with diverse partners about *kindergarten topics and text* cite details about conclusions drawn With prompting and support, ask and answer questions about key details |

| **CCSS Goals** | x | Vocabulary use | x | Answer real-world questions | x | Discuss, interpret, explain |
|---|---|---|---|---|---|---|
| | | Nonfiction use | x | Research | x | Collaboration |
| | x | Close reading | x | Build and present knowledge | x | Rigor |
| | x | Examine | x | Draw conclusions based on evidence | x | Relevance |

| | |
|---|---|
| **Rigor** | This lesson lends young minds an opportunity to observe and record details in order to draw conclusions. With guidance and support, learners will observe cause and effect relationships. |
| **Relevance** | Children love stories and this provides an opportunity to connect a story to our real-world. Personal voice and sharing observations fosters scientific thinking and confidence. Often stories reflect real-life issues and this story by Eric Carle gives us the opportunity to introduce "personification" as well as cause and effect relationships. Connecting mutual interdependence to the child's own experience, builds big ideas that go beyond the lesson. |

From *Think Tank Library: Brain-Based Learning Plans for New Standards, Grades K–5* by Paige Jaeger and Mary Boyd Ratzer. Santa Barbara, CA: Libraries Unlimited. Copyright © 2015.

| Listener and the task | Students will enjoy listening like a detective citing examples of how the sea community is inter-dependent in this story. After discussion and metacognitive modeling, learners can be asked to perform this task, which synthesizes vocabulary, theme of the book, cause and effect, and creativity, analyze and list their observations. |
|---|---|
| | • Students discuss the theme of the book (interdependency of community). |
| | • Students collaboratively discuss connections to real life. |
| | • Students share their observation with their class. |
| | • Students choose a character from the book and create a first person, personification, dialog of "how their natural ability or characteristics helped them meet their friend's need. |
| | • Students can dress up as their sea characters and talk about their role in helping. |
| | • Students speak and respond to questions using scientific vocabulary. |
| **Assessment** | Diagnostic assessment can be captured by asking the EQ's as listed above and noting answers. |
| | Summative assessment includes the same questions that now have answers. Summative assessment expects students to create paper or virtual knowledge products and summarizes new knowledge of how sea creatures use their strengths to survive and help others. Academic vocabulary as well as scientific vocabulary words should be present in sentences. |
| **Think Tank Spotlight** | This lesson engages the student to explore by asking questions. |
| | Students will learn by experience and observation. |
| | Students will synthesize how strengths compel actions. |
| | Students will strengthen their understanding of relationships. |
| | Students will be required to explain, using examples from the story. |

| Blooms Barometer | Remembering | Understanding | Applying | Analyzing | Evaluating | Creating |
|---|---|---|---|---|---|---|
| | x | x | x | x | x | x |

# Our Community: How Goods and Services Meet Wants and Needs                    Grades 1–2

## WHAT IS THE BIG IDEA?

As an outgrowth of a professional development in Gordon Creek Elementary in Ballston Spa, New York, this lesson was created, field-tested and was a huge success. This great group of innovative teachers used this lesson to experience Inquiry at its best. Community and parental involvement were the keys to success here and are usually present in your state teaching standards. Twenty-two community members volunteered to be interviewed for this project.

What's happening in the think tank when first graders explore their community through the lens of wants and needs and goods and service? With the school librarian as a key planner and facilitator, the class creates a walking tour. The class will map the community using digital photographs taken by the students and link them to interviews of local merchants and business owners. This inquiry-driven lesson starts with questions and ends with deep understanding. Students create a representation of their town by writing scripts from interviews of key community members and prepare for an open house where they personify the merchant or community member they interviewed. At this *community fair*, they present in character, tap their new knowledge, and answer questions. With a conceptual focus on the economics, needs, wants, resources, and citizens of their town, early elementary investigators can plan, generate questions, communicate, and document their learning on a long Know-Want to Know-Learned (KWL) chart in their classrooms or library.

## Potential Lesson Ideas shared by Kindergarten Teacher Liz Clancy, Gordon Creek Elementary:

- Journal writing: Draw and write about your community. (pre-assessment)
- Beginning map skills: What is a map?
  - Use building blocks to create a model of a town.
- Build the classroom community—How do jobs meet our wants and needs?
- A look at jobs
  - What is a job?
  - What type of jobs? What do they look like? How do they all work together? What type of tools would you use if you were a _____?
- Wonder box—artifact in a box (center or whole group): Prepare a box full of artifacts used by many who work or live in the community. Ask the students to think about the artifacts? Who would use it? Could it be used for anything else? Possible items in the wonder box: police badge, bowling pin, wrench, spatula, hair bower or scissors, dental pick, medicine bottle, deposit slip, stamps or mail bag, fire helmet, a copy of the Bible, ruler or sketch pad, menu, flower, flour or rolling pin, apron, chief's hat, library book...
- KWL or concept mapfor questions about jobs or places: What do they do? How do they support the community?
  - Photos of locations or workers within our school. (slide show) What do they do? Why are they here? How does this location/job helps the school run?
  - Community—(slide show) pictures of buildings and village streets. I wonder questions—I wonder what happens here? What type of jobs do they do here?
  - Share maps of the village—Google

- Journal writing. *Draw and write captions about a place you are interested in learning about.* Model and sample the I wonder questions—What do you want to know? "I wonder . . ."
- Go to the village field trip. Interact with local business personnel walk through parts of the village to observe building from the outside and possible enter and tour several places of business.
- Create a search strategy: What type of job would you like to do?
- What type of workplace would it be?—attire, what do I need to know, I can help the community by_____, describe the job you might want, what special types of tool would you need to work, uniform, training, what would your workplace look like?
- Location visits, about 10 minutes per location. Possible businesses may include: Bank, police, firehouse, bakery, park, village offices (mayor), (art gallery), library, bowling, auto body, mechanic, barber, gas station, food, kitchen, church, etc. (Who works here, how to help community, etc.)
- Journal writing. *Draw and write about a place in the community.* Create or prepare the diorama—uniform— to represent a way I might help my community
- Career day—parent and professionals come to school—knowledge presentation
- Write (journal entry), tell (presentation) and show (diorama to be displayed at the fair)
- Possible making and filming commercial about your location/job

| Lesson: | Our Community—How Goods and Services Meet Wants and Needs |
|---|---|
| Learning Targets: | Students investigate and record facts about their community by interviewing local merchants and service providers. Learners connect their own real-world to the new learning, making their prior knowledge transparent. As new facts consolidate into understanding, partial or incomplete information, misconceptions, and gaps in understanding transform into verifiable schema. |
| Essential Question | Why is my community important and how does it help me? |
| Guiding Questions: | Who are members of our community and why are they important? How does our community work together to meet wants and needs? How do community members provide goods and services to meet needs and wants? Where are the places that provide needed goods and service in my community? |
| Text | Books on community helpers, communities, towns, cities, and so on. Interviews of 22 local merchants recorded with video cameras or phones, by parent volunteers, and stored on the school's network space for access in the computer lab. Sample interview with the mayor conducted by the teacher, saved as a video. |
| Power words | Community, services, needs, wants, goods, merchant, producer, selling, buying |
| Vocabulary of library discipline | Investigate Question KWL Record Facts |

| CCSS Goals | x | Vocabulary use | x | Answer real-world questions | x | Discuss, interpret, explain |
|---|---|---|---|---|---|---|
| | x | Nonfiction use | x | Research | x | Collaboration |
| | | Close reading | x | Build and present knowledge | x | Rigor |
| | | Examine | | Evidence | x | Relevance |

| **Rigor** | This lesson turns a discussion about community into a real-life experience. With parent volunteers, students will construct their own community map-model from observations, digital photographs, direct experience, and spatial analysis. |
|---|---|
| **Relevance** | The community is the home of the learners. Some who live in a remote area travel to school by bus, and do not even know that there is a thriving village just beyond the school. Exploration of the town during a walking tour with digital cameras captures visual images and builds knowledge through experience. Personal voice and sharing new knowledge demonstrates the ultimate deep understanding. |
| **Listener and the task** | Students examine books and create lists of community members. Personal interest and choice initiates the process.<br>• Students analyze and list their wants and needs, and those of their family.<br>• Students organize facts, categorizing them into wants, needs, goods, and services using a KWL chart.<br>• Students collaboratively construct a map of their community using a shower curtain and digital photographs from a walking tour.<br>• Students generate questions for their investigations and interviews.<br>• Students write informative texts about their community using facts.<br>• Students produce and present descriptions of people, places, and things with relevant details, expressing ideas and feelings clearly.<br>• Students speak and respond to questions in the first person as the community member they interviewed, during an Open House Night, or lunch hour.<br>• Students listen to video camera recordings of their interviews, find, and chart important facts.<br>• First-hand experience, visual and graphical representation, collaboration with peers, and the construction of meaning insures formative knowledge and content mastery. |
| **Assessment** | Formative assessment can be captured using a concept map to sort facts and big ideas, or the giant KWL chart should document learning in this transparent manner. Assessment interviews with a checklist are a valuable way to determine whether a student can: categorizing, determine relationships, participate in discussions, identify cause and effects, and use the vocabulary of the community. Teachers and librarians can help review and edit questions for interviews. Summative assessment rubric of student script for Open House Night presentations works easily to document success. |

| Think Tank Spotlight | This lesson engages using prior knowledge regarding key concepts and asks them to explore by asking questions. This can be captured on a giant KWL chart where answers to questions (who, what, where, when) are organized. Students will learn by experience and will understand relationships and the reason for a community service or merchant. During this community investigation, students will be asked to compare and contrast, evaluate, and collaborate with peers to produce a knowledge product. This will require them to explains, use reason, communicate and express their knowledge. Worksheets with stick figures just cannot compare to this real-life learning endeavor. | | | | | |
|---|---|---|---|---|---|---|
| **Blooms Barometer** | Remembering<br>x | Understanding<br>x | Applying<br>x | Analyzing<br>x | Evaluating<br>x | Creating<br>x |
| **Standards Spotlight** | **National C3 Social Studies Standards—National Council for the Social Studies**<br>**The Inquiry Arc of the C3 Frameworks**<br>Suggested K–2 pathway for College, Career, and Civic Readiness<br>Dimension 2: Economics<br>Exchange and markets<br>Human Populations, Spatial Patterns and Movements<br>Construct maps and other representations of familiar places<br>Use maps, photographs and other representations to describe places and the relationships and interactions that shape them<br>Explain the goods and services that people in the local community produce and those that are produced in other communities<br>Describe goods and services that governments provide<br>Identify prices of products in a local market<br>Explain how people earn income<br>Describe examples of costs of production<br>Compare how people in different types of communities use local and distant environments to meet their daily needs<br>Describe the connections between the physical environment of a place and the economic activities found there<br><br>**Common Core**<br>Write informative/explanatory texts in which they name a topic, supply some facts about the topic, and provide some sense of closure.<br>Describe people, places, things, and events with relevant details, expressing ideas and feelings clearly.<br>Add drawings or other visual displays to descriptions when appropriate to clarify ideas, thoughts, and feelings.<br>Produce complete sentences when appropriate to task and situation.<br>Ask and answer questions about what a speaker says to gather additional information or clarify something that is not understood.<br>[© Copyright 2010. National Governors Association Center for Best Practices and Council of Chief State School Officers. All rights reserved.] | | | | | |

## Insect Investigations: Friend or Foe?                         Grades 1–2

## WHAT'S THE BIG IDEA?

While this lesson focuses on insects, we have a think-tank objective of introducing open-ended questioning. If we can teach a learner to wonder via open-ended questions, then we have triumphed early above rote and recall. All too often teachers give students hide and seek fact-fetching tasks, and the students hit the end thinking they have found all they need to know. In that model there is no deep discovery. Usually this task is followed by reporting insect trivia without any synthesis of the: *Why? So what? Or, why should I care?* This lesson will provide the opportunity for students to learn the first steps of Inquiry Based Learning by generating their own questions and get to a deeper understanding of entomology.

Using a question-starter we call the "Wonder Grid" (see graphics organizer), students will be able to ponder questions. The Wonder Grid can be used as a discussion tool or a graphic organizer (GO) depending upon student abilities. This is used to teach questioning and to determine what they need to discover to answer the essential question: *Is my insect friendly or fierce?* This simple essential question *requires* the student to synthesize the facts-found (evidence) to answer the task. Students will build an evidence-based claim (EBC) and discover that sometimes insects are both friend and foe. As long as a child can substantiate their claim with evidence, the rubric for assessment should provide them with a measurement of success.

This EBC knowledge product can be wrapped up nicely in many forms of technology. A simple Power-Point, Museum Box, Smore, or word-processed poster will provide the student with the opportunity to meet the Common Core ELA anchor standard: Research to build and present knowledge.

| Lesson: | Insect: Friend or Foe? Grades 1–2 |
|---|---|
| Learning Targets: | Students will learn to ask open-ended questions. Students will use credible databases to investigate answers. Students will speak using vocabulary of the research discipline. Students will practice speaking with text-based answers. Students will learn about insects and demonstrate their learning speaking with content-specific vocabulary. |
| Essential Questions | Are insects friendly? Or, are they our "foe?" Friendly or Fierce? |
| Guiding questions: | How can we determine whether this helps us or hurts us? How can we use a credible database to investigate answers? Do insects play a vital role in our food chain? How might insects help us or our world? Could it be possible that an insect is both friendly and fierce? Can you support that idea? |
| Text | *Fiction:* *Explorer Extraordinaire!* by Jane O'Connor (Fancy Nancy-great vocabulary) *Face Bugs* by J. Patrick Lewis *Big Bug Surprise*, by Julia Gran *I Love Bugs* by Philemon Sturges *Superworm* by Julia Donaldson |

| | |
|---|---|
| | *Be Nice to Spiders*, Margaret Bloy Graham<br>*It's a Good Thing There Are Insects* by Allen Fowler.<br><br>Non-fiction low level insect books<br>Low-level Encyclopedia such as: World Book Online Kids<br>Databases such as PebbleGo, Kids InfoBits, and others suitable for Grades 1–2 |
| **Power words** | Insect Bodies: three body parts, four wings, six legs, thorax, abdomen, antenna<br>Insect Homes: cocoon, colony, hive<br>Insect Life Cycles: egg, grub, larva<br>Other: exoskeleton, compound eye, chrysalis, nectar, pollen, and additional academic words that you may find within each chosen book |
| **Vocabulary of library discipline** | Keywords, evidence, investigate, claim, source, credible, open-ended questions, wonder questions |

| **CCSS Goals** | x | Vocabulary use | x | Solve real-world issues | x | Discuss, interpret, explain, debate |
|---|---|---|---|---|---|---|
| | x | Nonfiction use | x | Research | x | Use formal English |
| | x | Close reading | x | Build and present knowledge | x | Rigor |
| | x | Evidence-based Claim | x | Investigate | x | Relevance |

| | |
|---|---|
| **Rigor** | By requiring students to use the vocabulary of the discipline in their knowledge product, you are demanding synthesis and understanding. This is a new task for these children and yet with guidance they can experience success. Brain research says we underestimate the ability of a young child to assimilate difficult vocabulary and this provides us a challenge to embrace. Science words should be modeled aloud ahead of time providing the correct pronunciation and decoding visual. This will get the words into a student's "receptive" vocabulary. In their knowledge product we aim to find these same words in their "productive" vocabulary, demonstrating mastery of the domain-specific vocabulary. Another element of rigor to require is the open-ended rigor questions. By requiring both yes-no and open-ended, the child will experience the difference.<br>Assignment: Working alone or with a partner allows the teacher the ability to differentiate the task for challenged learners as well as gifted learners. If a child completes his investigation early, you can challenge him to create the "other side of the argument" and create a second EBC. Create five fact questions. Create five open-ended questions to investigate. |
| **Relevance** | Bugs are all around us, and by nature are a relevant part of our world.<br>If you tap into emotions by asking students if they have ever been misunderstood, you will get their attention and make a connection to the insect investigation on which they are about to embark. |
| **Reader and the task** | Classroom brainstorming of insects or bugs on a graffiti wall, whiteboard, or other mind-storming tool provides the class with an opportunity to contribute.<br><br>Insect Immersion—Collaboration stations with insect books will provide a platform for deeper discovery. Teachers can choose to go over the power words ahead of time with |

From *Think Tank Library: Brain-Based Learning Plans for New Standards, Grades K–5* by Paige Jaeger and Mary Boyd Ratzer. Santa Barbara, CA: Libraries Unlimited. Copyright © 2015.

students, or give them the opportunity to create their word wall themselves. This simple task gives them ownership of the content and they are likely to take it more seriously. An effective model is to "start" the wall with a few domain-specific words, modeling importance and pronunciation, and then ask them to complete the wall.

Students choose an insect to investigate. Possible choices are: ant, bee, beetle, butterfly, caterpillar, centipede, cockroach, cricket, dragonfly, flea, fly, honeybee, grasshopper, grub, ladybug, maggot, mosquito, moth, spider, termite, tick, wasp, or any other insect they discover in the insect immersion. That might be as far as you get for the first step of this project.

Insect Investigation—Using a GO, students collect evidence for their helpful or hinder charts, guiding the students with questions, help them synthesize their information to draw a conclusion on whether this is a friend or foe.

Insectlopedia—Students create either via paper or virtual Web tool, an insect museum ("Insectlopedia" "Insectarium") and organize the bugs into two or three classifications: Friends, Foe, and Further Thinking Required

Innovative knowledge products such as "Wanted Posters" for perilous insects may stand juxtapose next to "Helping Hero" posters. In some cases, you might find a group wanting to create both a WANTED poster as well as a Helping Hero poster for the same creature.

Students should be given the opportunity to share their knowledge, as the CCSS requires in "research to build and *present* knowledge."

This research endeavor supports non-fiction reading (CCSS objectives) and text-based answers (CCSS objectives) With the knowledge product in mind, students have a purpose (an engaged task) and this transfers "ownership" to the student.

Differentiation possibilities would include replicating the Face Bug poem from Lewis's book. This would challenge those needing learning extensions. Learning extensions can include discussion and debate or creating an action plan for a troubled insect or problem that may have been discovered during investigation.

| | |
|---|---|
| **Assessment** | Students choose an insect for investigation.<br>• Graphic organizers work well at this age to guide the students.<br>• Students investigate positive and negative influential human interactions and complete their GOs with facts<br>• Graphic Organizers can be used as a guide for finishing the task as well as insuring that the expectations for "evidence (i.e., facts) are met. |
| **Think Tank Spotlight** | This lesson places the student at the center of his learning. Giving him a decision to make empowers him to learn. In requiring, the student to make an assessment of "friend or foe" requires synthesis of facts found. It embraces cause and effect of scientific thinking. It incubates the idea of hypothesis and support. Using the vocabulary of the discipline will require understanding of the content. Learners creating an evidence-based-claim and are ready to justify their label of friend or foe. They have reached the top of Blooms and beyond. Not bad for a first grader. |

| **Blooms Barometer** | Remembering | Understanding | Applying | Analyzing | Evaluating | Creating |
|---|---|---|---|---|---|---|
| | x | x | x | x | x | x |

| Standards Spotlight | **Common Core**<br>• Vocabulary use, engaged dialogue,<br>• Research to build and present knowledge,<br>• Evidence (information) based claim, collaborative workgroups, solve real-world problems.<br>• Speaking and Listening Standards: Discuss, interpret, explain, present claims and findings,<br>• Use formal English<br>  [© Copyright 2010. National Governors Association Center for Best Practices and Council of Chief State School Officers. All rights reserved.] |

This Wonder Grid, which follows, originally created by a local elementary librarian, helps students learn the art of asking open-ended questions. This may prove helpful at any grade level to prompt questions leading to Inquiry. Notice the opportunity to craft both open-ended as well as concrete questions. Some local libraries have had these prompts stenciled on their walls to inspire Inquiry.

| I wonder . . . | Define | How . . . |
| --- | --- | --- |
| What | Describe | What if . . . |
| When | Which | Should . . . |
| How | Identify | Why . . . |
| Who | Where | Could . . . |
| Explain | Which | Would . . . |
| Compare | Predict | Is there . . . |

# SPOTLIGHT ON THINKING- GRADE 2

Second graders have made giant steps in their cognitive development worthy of spotlighting here. They exhibit confidence in what they can do and what they know. Confident and often aware of other's feelings, they use their emerging skills and social intelligence. Seconds grade thinkers:

- Expands vocabulary by reading and talking, adding to fluency
- Listen and retain information that is heard
- Listen actively and participate in groups
- Understand information that is read in multiple texts
- Follows multiple step directions
- Focus on tasks longer
- Develop individual learning style
- Have a need to know and ask questions
- Plan with multiple steps
- Ask questions to understand more clearly or deeply
- Answer questions with multiple information sources
- Solve problems with creative and complex solutions
- Use logic to solve problems
- Identify and solve problems using the views of others
- Connect concepts to experience
- Locate facts and information
- Compares and contrasts objects
- Sequence events in a basic order, write narratives that recount actions
- Support opinions with reasons
- Make decisions with confidence
- Predict and then test their ideas
- Observe the world and make predictions based on what is observed
- Discuss thinking when solving math problems
- Ascribe characteristics to what is observed
- Reflects on thinking

Take time to assess your lessons to insure you are tapping into the correct cognitive development of the emerging reader. Instructional time is too valuable to waste by not challenging our students. Use a highlighter and highlight items on the list above to give yourself credit for what you've embraced, as well as identify what you can target. Be sure to note cognitive targets in your educational portfolio or identify these in your observations.

## Put Me in the Zoo                                       Grades 2–3

## WHAT'S THE BIG IDEA?

What's happening in the think tank when second graders explore animals in their natural habitats, and compare that to life in captivity? The class will create a picture zoo with signage to demonstrate the synthesis of facts found at their *community zoo*, they present their new knowledge, and answer questions. Early elementary investigators can plan, generate questions, communicate, and document their learning in the library.

A technology transfer would be to create this zoo virtually on a web page, using a map of a local zoo linking *Blabberize, Audacity* files to "spots" (Thinglink) on the map. Zoo visitors could click on the spots and hear the voice of the animals giving advice to the zookeepers. (A plethora of other web tools exist for this application such as GarageBand, Museum Box, and others that your school may favor.)

The big idea of this lesson is to transform the old "animal report" into something asking your students to synthesize. Most animal reports around the country are lower-level mere transfer of information. The teacher-librarian who piloted this project remarked:

> I can already see the students approaching this project with greater thought when given the task of giving their animals a voice. One student who is researching Peregrine Falcons said to me, "Mrs. Abad, if I was a peregrine falcon I wouldn't sleep very much." I thought this was kind of an odd statement, so I asked him to explain. He said, "I wouldn't sleep because owls and eagles would be trying to eat me at night."
>
> I think this is a great example of how that essential question is getting them to engage in that higher level thinking. Instead of just copying down the animal's enemies, he was actually thinking about the impact it would have on his animal.

In our field-testing locations, we actually asked librarians to use old fashioned index cards for facts—one fact per card. This was helpful in helping students synthesize facts into meaning. They were able to sort into categories such as cause and effect, habitat, and so on. Later elementary students, who move to online note-cards, will have the basis of understanding of what the online version is doing for them. We found that physically begin able to sort facts into groups, helped the connections made in synthesis.

Examine your current "animal reports" against this lesson that incubates higher-level thought.

| Lesson: | Put Me in the Zoo |
|---|---|
| Learning Targets: | Students investigate and record facts about their animal synthesizing facts into meaningful big ideas or concepts. Students will learn how to use a credible online database resources such as Capstone Pebble Go or another encyclopedia Learners connect their own real-world to the new learning, making their prior knowledge transparent. As new facts consolidate into understanding, partial or incomplete information, misconceptions, gaps in understanding, and transforms. |
| Essential Questions: | If you were sending your animal to The [Bronx] Zoo, what advice would your animal give the zookeeper? What should the sign on his cage read? |

| Guiding Questions: | How can we make meaning of facts? Can we synthesize? Where can we find credible information? What makes your animal unique? Who would your animal fear? What would your animal fear? | | | | | |
|---|---|---|---|---|---|---|
| Text | Hook Book of your choices such as nonfiction books on animals. Online information resource of your choice such as PebbleGo or World Book Online | | | | | |
| Power words | Habitat, ecosystem, prey, predator, carnivore, herbivore, omnivore, camouflage, defense, diet, appearance, adaptations, survival, enemies, etc. | | | | | |
| Vocabulary of library discipline | Investigate, question, notes, own words (paraphrase) record facts, synthesize, | | | | | |
| CCSS Goals | x | Vocabulary use | x | Answer real-world questions | x | Discuss, interpret, explain |
| | x | Nonfiction use | x | Research | x | Collaboration |
| | x | Close reading | x | Build and present knowledge | x | Rigor |
| | x | Text-based answers | x | Investigate | x | Relevance |
| Rigor | This lesson turns an old fact-finding model into a synthesis endeavor aligned with national science goals. Students need to metacognitively see cause and effect relationships and draw conclusions. | | | | | |
| Relevance | With the innate primary interest in animals, student choice will be used as a tool for engagement. Personal voice and sharing new knowledge demonstrates the ultimate deep understanding. Collaborative work and social interaction while planning, investigating, or sharing transform a learning experience with ownership and investment. | | | | | |
| Reader Listener and the task | The "tasks" for animal research can take many sizes and shapes, and this lesson suggestion is just one of many alternatives which move beyond "reporting" animal facts. Writing in the first-person voice of the animal requires synthesis of facts to apply their new knowledge. Moving beyond a "written report" to a showcase of knowledge also validates the learning. Speaking and listening standards encourage students the present their knowledge. A virtual zoo, or paper presentations will allow students practice in fluency, thought, and supporting a claim with evidence. | | | | | |
| Assessment | Students will be able to articulate what concerns they have for their animal. Students can speak using the vocabulary of the discipline Students have produced an evidence based claim synthesizing their animal facts into a concern. | | | | | |

| Think Tank Spotlight | • Have a need to know and ask questions<br>• Solve problems with creative and complex solutions<br>• Support opinions with reasons<br>• Locate facts and information<br>• Reflects on thinking<br>• Connect concepts to experience<br>• Expands vocabulary by reading and talking, adding to fluency<br>• Listen and retain information that is heard<br>• Understand information that is read in multiple texts<br>• Answer questions with multiple information sources<br>• Make decisions with confidence | | | | | |
|---|---|---|---|---|---|---|
| Blooms Barometer | Remembering<br>x | Understanding<br>x | Applying<br>x | Analyzing<br>x | Evaluating<br>x | Creating<br>x |
| Standards Spotlight | **National Science Standards**<br>Planning and carrying out investigations to answer questions or test solutions to problems in K-2 builds on prior experiences and progresses to simple investigations, based on fair tests, which provide data to support explanations or design solutions.<br>Plan and conduct an investigation collaboratively to produce data to serve as the basis for evidence to answer a question.<br>Copyright 2013 Achieve, Inc. All rights reserved<br><br>**Common Core**<br>Write informative/explanatory texts in which they name a topic, supply some facts about the topic, and provide some sense of closure.<br>Describe people, places, things, and events with relevant details, expressing ideas and feelings clearly.<br>Add drawings or other visual displays to descriptions when appropriate to clarify ideas, thoughts, and feelings.<br>Produce complete sentences when appropriate to task and situation.<br>Ask and answer questions about what a speaker says to gather additional information or clarify something that is not understood.<br>[© Copyright 2010. National Governors Association Center for Best Practices and Council of Chief State School Officers. All rights reserved.] | | | | | |

| *Power Words* | *Power Words* | *Power Words* |
|---|---|---|
| These are words you are likely to read, find, and discover when you investigate your animals. They are the keys to understanding what your animal is all about. | These are words you are likely to read, find, and discover when you investigate your animals. They are the keys to understanding what your animal is all about. | These are words you are likely to read, find, and discover when you investigate your animals. They are the keys to understanding what your animal is all about. |
| We expect you to use these words within your animal projects. | We expect you to use these words within your animal projects. | We expect you to use these words within your animal projects. |

| | | |
|---|---|---|
| Adaptations | Adaptations | Adaptations |
| Appearance | Appearance | Appearance |
| Camouflage | Camouflage | Camouflage |
| Carnivore | Carnivore | Carnivore |
| Defense | Defense | Defense |
| Diet | Diet | Diet |
| Diet | Diet | Diet |
| Ecosystem | Ecosystem | Ecosystem |
| Enemies | Enemies | Enemies |
| Herbivore | Herbivore | Herbivore |
| Life Cycle | Life Cycle | Life Cycle |
| Omnivore | Omnivore | Omnivore |
| Predator | Predator | Predator |
| Prey | Prey | Prey |
| Survival | Survival | Survival |

CHAPTER 16

# THE LATE ELEMENTARY DISCOVERY GRADES (3–5) LIBRARY AND CLASSROOM LESSONS

## How Does a Rock Tell the History of Earth?                                          Grade 3

### Narrative Writing in Science

> *Contrary to older views, young children are not concrete and simplistic thinkers. Research shows that children's thinking is surprisingly sophisticated. Children can use a wide range of reasoning processes that form the underpinnings of scientific thinking, even though their experience is variable and they have much more to learn.*
>
>                         Duschl, Schweingruber, & Shouse, *Taking Science to School*. Washington, D.C. National
>                                                                                         Academies Press. 2007, pp. 2–3

## WHAT'S THE BIG IDEA?

Elementary learners in Grade 3 bring experience of their world and innate curiosity to school every day. Countless rock collectors, rock throwers, and rock finders belong to the ranks of third graders. This lesson turns these budding geologists into thinkers via Inquiry. Observations, recording data and facts, and collaboratively uncovering explanations stimulate thinking. Questions, hypotheses, and a learner-centered investigation engage learners in geology.

   The inquiry cycle begins with prior knowledge and experience. Narratives, poetry, and nonfiction books, pictures, and databases such as *PebbleGo* and *Brain Pop Junior*, build background and introduce scientific facts. At this stage the learner develops the vocabulary and conceptual ideas to think about rocks as evidence of the history of the earth. Children explore rocks in the classroom, share their own collections, wonder about them, question, and share. Guided inquiry proceeds as questions are identified and charted that might be investigated. Learners explore and predict, plan, collect, and record data. Learners organize, categorize, look for relationships, and draw conclusions from facts. Critical thinking and information literacy merge. This overarching essential question raises the level of thinking: *How does a rock tell us the history of the earth?*

These are both online information tools for connected libraries. Visit BrainPop.com or PebbleGo.com

Ultimately scientific knowledge of geology will be used and applied in the knowledge product. Using a storyboard for organization, students will produce a narrative that tells the story of a rock of their choice. Geographic context and change over time, cause and effect of water, weather, volcanoes, and other forces will frame a setting and a sequence of events for the rock's story. Even predictions for the future of the rock could be considered. The Common Core Standards and Next Generation Science Standards posit the importance of explaining science in narratives.

If a student understands the science deeply, the main ideas of the rock's origin, change over time, inter-action with natural forces, movement, and composition become the framework of a story. Evidence acquired through investigation support the main idea, and become the supporting details illustrating the rock-story and its vast time span. Visuals and drawings enhance the science and the story. Sharing these knowledge products is a scientific synthesis of many geological understandings. The world is making sense through science, reading, writing, and creativity.

| Lesson: | How Does a Rock Tell the History of Earth? |
|---|---|
| Learning Targets: | *Students know, use, and interpret scientific explanations of the natural world.* *Students generate and evaluate scientific evidence and explanations.* *Students participate productively in scientific practices* (Heidi Schweingruber Board on Science Education, The National Academies, 2007). Students collaboratively inquire and develop explanations and ideas. • Students wonder, notice, ask questions, observe. • Students compare, explore, investigate, and record information. • Students predict, plan, analyze facts and experiences, and formulate evidence. • Students think, debate, discuss, write, communicate, and share. • Students read for information, identify main ideas and supporting details. • Students draw conclusions and create a narrative of the *Life Story of a Rock.* Students write narratives to develop real or imagined experiences or events using effective technique, descriptive details, and clear event sequences. |
| Essential Questions: | How does a rock tell the history of Earth? |
| Guiding Questions: | How do rocks form? How are rocks categorized into types? What forces change rocks over time? Why does geography determine a rock's life story? How old are rocks? Why do rocks have different appearances and properties? How can the geology of the earth reveal clues about the history of the earth? |
| Text | *The Big Rock* by Bruce Hiscock *Earthshake: Poems from the Ground Up* by Lisa Westberg Peters *Eruption!* By Elizabeth Rusch USGS: Collecting Rocks by Rachel Barker http://pubs.usgs.gov/gip/collect1/collectgip.html Mineralogical Society of America http://www.mineralogy4kids.org/ *B is for Blue Planet: An Earth Science Alphabet* by Ruth Strother *If You Find a Rock* by Peggy Christian Databases that your school may subscribe to such as Scholastic ScienceFlix or TrueFlix; eLibrary, Kids InfoBits or others Other resources you find on your library shelves and or subscribe to online |

| Power words | Metamorphic, sedimentary, igneous, lava, magma, fossil, rock cycle, weathering, erosion, sediment, clay, granite, quartz, landforms, minerals, geology, shale, slate, sandstone, glaciers, earth's crust, meteorites |
|---|---|
| **Vocabulary of library discipline** | Observe, hypothesize, investigate, analyze, evidence, main idea, supporting details, narrative, scientific thinking, predictions, debate, conclusions, record |

| CCSS Goals | x | Vocabulary use | x | Solve real-world issues | x | Discuss, interpret, explain |
|---|---|---|---|---|---|---|
| | x | Nonfiction use | x | Research | x | Use formal English |
| | x | Close reading | x | Build and present knowledge | x | Rigor |
| | x | Evidence-Based Claim | x | Text-Based Answers | x | Relevance |

| **Rigor** | Rigorous work in science requires diligence and critical thinking to find truth. Children's thinking regarding scientific topics can be robustly inaccurate. Old ideas need to be modified by new knowledge. Scientific information sources challenge readers with vocabulary and concepts that far out distance what a child can see or hear or experience. The history of planet Earth as told through geology extends far back in time. Learners need to think about and apply understanding of complex forces that work over time.

Constructing a sequenced storyboard of the life history of a rock needs a strong basis in fact, which is quite a shift from fairytales and the Disney *Ice Age* world. Accurate and plausible fact is the foundation for their creative account. This involves convergent and divergent thinking—What if? Teachers become the learning concierge they need to make sense of details discovered to tell a story using the vocabulary of the discipline—collaborating, speaking, listening, writing, expressing, and demonstrating content mastery. |
|---|---|
| **Relevance** | The common rock, ubiquitous, always underfoot, can be ignored. However, curious collectors, rock-tossing enthusiasts, wonderers, and those closer to the ground tend to note them, pick them, save them, and ask questions about them. This common experience serves as the platform for relevance. Understanding the world around them is ultimately relevant, as children learn how to turn natural curiosity into a learning experience. |
| **Reader and the task** | • Readers will record information and scientific facts, categorizing them into main ideas and supporting details.<br>• Reading with a purpose characterizes this inquiry quest.<br>• Equipping each learner with the vocabulary and key ideas of the science, sets the learning process in motion.<br>• Readers identify, access, and use multiple information sources.<br>• Text features guide to important and useful information.<br>• Use of databases, animation and video, and pictures varies information formats.<br>• Sharing and collaborating, learners will determine useful texts and construct meaning.<br>• Questions, KWL charts, and graphic organizers will sustain the process of building explanations that are rooted in science. From the graphic organizers students can creatively express knowledge in written narratives. |

| Assessment | Formative: |
|---|---|
| |     Discussion and charting |
| |     KWL Charts |
| |     Think Pair Share |
| |     Main ideas and supporting details—graphic organizer |
| |     Storyboard for organization |
| |     Writing drafts with conferencing |
| |     Storyboard checklist, peer review |
| | Summative: |
| |     Rubric for narrative writing based on science |
| **Think Tank Spotlight** | Use open ended questions: |
| |     What do you think, wonder? |
| |     What do you see? Feel? |
| |     What do you think happened? |
| |     Why does that happen? |
| |     How can you tell? |
| |     Why is this different? |
| | Questions move from a groundwork of facts to HOW, WHY, SHOULD, WHAT IF |
| | Multiple perspectives enhance understanding, and factor into close reading and writing |
| | Multiple causes and multiple effects can be understood and manipulated |
| | Long-term and immediate causes and effects can be distinguished |
| | Change over time can be discerned and represented |
| | Relationships among patterns and processes are recognized |
| | Different forms of evidence are analyzed and used to construct meaning |
| | Integrating information from sources is increasingly based on evaluation of that information |
| | Support of opinions employs grouping ideas |
| | Reasoning is increasingly based on supporting facts and details |
| | Use of evidence from texts along with reflection supports research |
| | Self-awareness about thinking and learning develops |
| | Metacognition becomes more sophisticated and productive |
| | Focus is increasingly key to performance in complex tasks, writing, and communicating |
| | Linking ideas within and across categories employs language that makes distinctions |
| | Logic in ordering ideas increasingly demands reflection and analysis |
| | Drawing conclusions from information and knowledge is genuine synthesis |
| | Expanding and structured networks in the brain facilitate retention of new knowledge |
| | Organization of mental tasks becomes faster and more extensively used |
| | Prior knowledge makes new knowledge easier to store in long-term memory |
| | Subject area expertise impacts speed and continued new knowledge acquisition |
| | Memory strategies begin to support new learning |

| **Blooms Barometer** | Remembering | Understanding | Applying | Analyzing | Evaluating | Creating |
|---|---|---|---|---|---|---|
| | x | x | x | x | x | x |

| **Standards Spotlight** | **Next Generation Science Standards-Grades 3–5** |
|---|---|
| | • **Earth Materials and Systems** |
| |     Rainfall helps to shape the land and affects the types of living things found in a region. Water, ice, wind, living organisms, and gravity break rocks, soils, and sediments into smaller particles and move them around. |

From *Think Tank Library: Brain-Based Learning Plans for New Standards, Grades K–5* by Paige Jaeger and Mary Boyd Ratzer. Santa Barbara, CA: Libraries Unlimited. Copyright © 2015.

- **Cause and Effect**
  Cause and effect relationships are routinely identified, tested, and used to explain change.
- **Analyzing and Interpreting Data**
  Obtain and combine information from books and other reliable media to explain phenomena.
- Copyright 2013 Achieve, Inc. All rights reserved

**Common Core Standards**
**ELA/Literacy**
- Ask and answer questions to demonstrate understanding of a text, referring explicitly to the text as the basis for the answers.
- Compare and contrast the most important points and key details presented in two texts on the same topic.
- Recall information from experiences or gather information from print and digital sources; take brief notes on sources and sort evidence into provided categories.

**Writing Text Type and Purposes**
- Write narratives to develop real or imagined experiences or events using effective technique, descriptive details, and clear event sequences.
- Establish a situation and introduce a narrator and/or characters; organize an event sequence that unfolds naturally.
- Use dialogue and descriptions of actions, thoughts, and feelings to develop experiences and events or show the response of characters to situations.
- Use temporal words and phrases to signal event order.

**Production and Distribution of Writing:**
- With guidance and support from adults, produce writing in which the development and organization are appropriate to task and purpose. (Grade-specific expectations for writing types are defined in Standards 1–3 above.)

[© Copyright 2010. National Governors Association Center for Best Practices and Council of Chief State School Officers. All rights reserved.]

## How Are These Related?                                 Grades 3–4

## WHAT IS THE BIG IDEA? 1–2 LESSONS

The objective is to hit the synthesis target helping students to *make connections regarding relationships in seemingly disparate ideas.* If your library has iPads, or you are in a 1-to-1 school with devices, you may wish to consider this lesson to integrate the iPads into your instruction. This gives you the opportunity to use the devices as more than a portable computer to help find books.

This short one session lesson is meant to activate thinking and support the cause and effect standard being taught in the classroom. "Mentor texts" for cause and effect are abundant. If your students are reading an ELA novel with an obvious cause and effect theme, such as *11 Birthdays* by Wendy Mass, it is easy to tie into classroom activities. Otherwise there are a great number of picture books that serve to model this standard listed in the lesson plan such as *Cloudy With a Chance of Meatballs,* or *Why Mosquitoes Buzz in People's Ears.* Examine the mentor texts and choose examples that have valuable vocabulary as well as cause and effect relationships to embrace the CCSS vocabulary shift.

After reading a mentor text for cause and effect, or connecting to a classroom core novel with cause and effect examples, have students work in collaborative groups at tables with iPads or devices with previously downloaded apps listed in the chart below. A sample essential question would be, "How are these two apps relevant to our conversations about *11 Birthdays?*

These engaging apps have no real connection to the cause and effect texts. When you ask students to synthesize possible connections, you are asking them to think outside the box and outside their comfort zone. They are forced to synthesize possible connections.

When local librarian, Susan Kirby-Lemon, of Skano Elementary School, Clifton Park, NY, shared this activity, she said the metacognitive change in her students was "visible":

*"Talk about looks of cognitive discomfort! It took them a few minutes and some modeling to think about what happened. . .They did get there eventually, and here are some of their deep thoughts":*

- Time seems to stop when you hold the screen, as it did in the book.
- The harder you press in Fluid, the bigger the ripple. Leo said a really mean thing about Amanda, so it had a big ripple. (This observation got us to cause and effect, which served as our metacognitive modeling.)
- When I push down on the screen, the fish swim away, like when Amanda and Leo are apart for the year. Something has pushed them apart—the fight has pushed them apart.
- The life of the fish is always the same unless I do something to the screen. Amanda and Leo's lives were the same because they kept repeating until the end when they made up. Then it was the same as it was before in a good way.
- When you tap the fish, you may hurt them, like Leo hurt Amanda.
- The baby fish are important in the app because they grow, just like Angelina DeAngelo was important to the babies when they were born. She was important to how they grew up.

The connection to the classroom novel is a great way to model the library as an achievement partnership. Teachers worried about their Annual Professional Performance Review (APPR) ratings will likely be grateful for your contribution supporting their objectives.

| Lesson: | How Are These Related?—Investigating Cause and Effect |
|---|---|
| **Learning Targets:** | Students will connect the iPad apps to the story<br>Students will speak using examples (evidence) from the story to support their connection<br>Students will practice speaking with text-based answers<br>Students will make a cause and effect connection<br>Students will synthesize two seemingly unrelated ideas |
| **Essential Questions:** | Can we identify cause and effect?<br>Can we make connections between these apps and our book?<br>How are the book and this app connected? |
| **Mentor Text(s)** | *11 Birthdays*, by Wendy Mass<br>*Grandpa's Teeth*, by Clement<br>*The Day the Cow Sneezed*, by Flora<br>*Dream Wolf*, by Goble<br>*On Monday When it Rained*, by Kachenmeister<br>*Pecos Bill*, by Kellogg<br>*Rabbit Stew*, by Kosow<br>*The Day That Jimmy's Boa Ate the Wash*, by Noble<br>*If You Give a [Mouse] a Cookie*, by Numeroff<br>Many more that you may enjoy, but pick those with academic vocabulary |
| **Technology** | *Two iPad apps were used for this lesson*<br>*Pocket Pond 2 (free app)*<br>*Fluid (free app)*<br>If you have no devices, you may choose to bring in toys that have a cause and effect relationship. Each table could serve as a station where kids have to make connections between the story and the toy. |
| **Power words** | Choose vocabulary words from any picture book that you may read. You may wish to choose a specific book that has valuable vocabulary within. These words power words from *Cloudy With a Chance of Meatballs*:<br>    Abandon, absolute, accompany, assort, brief, ceiling, chew and swallow, consist, continue, damage, decision, drift, event, frequent, gradual, hurricane, incident, menu, necessity, object, occasion, predict, realize, sanitation, supply, surround, survive, tall tale, temporary, tornado, violent<br>By including some simpler words, you are instilling confidence for students who made need that reassurance. |
| **Vocabulary of library discipline** | synthesize, evidence, cause, effect, support |

| **CCSS Goals** | x | Vocabulary use | | Solve real-world issues | x | Discuss, interpret, explain, debate, |
|---|---|---|---|---|---|---|
| | | Nonfiction use | | Research | x | Use formal English |

From *Think Tank Library: Brain-Based Learning Plans for New Standards, Grades K–5* by Paige Jaeger and Mary Boyd Ratzer. Santa Barbara, CA: Libraries Unlimited. Copyright © 2015.

| | x | Close reading | | Build and present knowledge | x | Rigor |
|---|---|---|---|---|---|---|
| | x | Evidence-Based Claim | x | Investigate | x | Relevance |

| | |
|---|---|
| **Rigor** | Try to choose a mentor text that embraces robust vocabulary so that you are weaving in more than one objective of the CC. |
| **Relevance** | By integrating technology and making connections to toys, iPads, and previously read books, this content is instantly relevant to the student's world. This lesson heightens the value and relevance of print to a generation loving technology.<br>As a hook, you can brainstorm cause and effect scenarios that students may be familiar with such as<br>• If you eat a great deal of candy and don't brush your teeth, you'll?<br>• If you forget to close the front door in wintertime, you'll ___? ___<br>• If you don't take a bath for days, you'll likely ___? |
| **Reader and the task** | • EQ: Can we read like a detective and identify cause and effect relationships? This lesson could be preceded by a station-rotation lesson where collaborative teams rotate tables, each table having different "cause and effect" picture book mentor texts. The cause and effect GO could be used for the students to closely read the text(s) for cause and effect relationships.<br>(See example.)<br>• At each table provide a device with access to free apps such as Fluid or Pocket Pond 2. Each has an interactive water setting, in one you feed and play with Koi, the other is just a liquid surface. The focus question could be: How are these two apps relevant to our conversations regarding *11 Birthdays*? The task was: Convince the group of any connection(s) using textual evidence to support your ideas. |
| **Assessment** | Student self-assessment bookmarks are recommended. Students would use these as a guide for finishing the task as well as insuring that the expectations are met. Expectations for an exemplary knowledge product are listed and checked off.<br>See the following example: |
| **Think Tank Spotlight** | • Expanding knowledge creates a platform for meaning with new information<br>• Chunking information on the basis of connections moves beyond concrete categories<br>• Reasoning is increasingly based on supporting facts and details<br>• Use of evidence from texts along with reflection supports research<br>• Metacognition becomes more sophisticated and productive<br>• Focus is increasingly key to performance in complex tasks, writing, and communicating<br>• Planning and goal setting evolve from amateur to apprentice<br>• Tools for self-assessment boost progress and performance<br>• Questions move from a groundwork of facts to HOW, WHY, SHOULD, WHAT IF<br>• Long-term and immediate causes and effects can be distinguished<br>• Integrating information from sources is increasingly based on evaluation of that information<br>• Linking ideas within and across categories employs language that makes distinctions<br>• Drawing conclusions from information and knowledge is genuine synthesis<br>• Organization of mental tasks becomes faster and more extensively used |

| Blooms Barometer | Remembering<br>x | Understanding<br>x | Applying<br>x | Analyzing<br>x | Evaluating<br>x | Creating<br>x |
|---|---|---|---|---|---|---|
| Standards Spotlight | **Common Core**<br>• Speaking and Listening Standards: Discuss, interpret, explain, present claims and findings, use formal English<br>• Research to build and present knowledge<br>• Use formal English<br>• Apply knowledge of language to understand how language functions in different contexts, to make effective choices for meaning or style, and to comprehend more fully when reading or listening.<br>• Discuss, explain, present claims and findings, use formal English and more<br>   [© Copyright 2010. National Governors Association Center for Best Practices and Council of Chief State School Officers. All rights reserved.] | | | | | |

**Sample graphic organizer for picture book station rotation stations:**

| Book Title | Cause (Cite example from the text) Please indicate page # | Effect (Cite example from the text) Please indicate page # |
|---|---|---|
| | | |
| | | |
| | | |
| Brainstorm a book you're reading on your own . . . Can you think of a cause and effect within that book? | | |

# Wacky-World Problems                 Grades 4–5

## WHAT'S THE BIG IDEA?

Creative possibilities are endless—even within the Common Core instruction. As you get to know the building blocks of rigor you will see it is easy to and embrace them and challenge students to think. If you were observed during this lesson, the principal would likely see your students concentrating on: vocabulary, building an evidence-based claim, researching to build and present knowledge, and closely reading. That is what separates you from a granny reading a nice book. Plan your pedagogy. Engage those students in reading, research, and academic vocabulary building.

Whether you collaborate with a classroom teacher spotlighting community, or do this lesson during your scheduled library time, you can teach CCSS style. You do not have to be a classroom teacher. If you try this *wacky-world problems unit*, you are embracing many of the shifts of the Common Core which have been carefully woven together. After your students read this book, they are likely to know 20 more academic vocabulary words than they did prior to reading this book.

This unit goes on to incubate problem-solving skills at an early age. You can build a rubric, which requires them to use the power words in their evidence-based claim. You could have a discussion and debate over real-world issues, citing evidence. This can be part of their writing or language presentation. Students move from listening to investigating, solving problems, and speaking with evidence.

This lesson strives to metacognitively model thinking. When students who cannot think, hear thinking out loud, they learn to think. This lesson asks higher level thought questions such as: What problems deserve governmental attention the most? Which problem should be solved first? The identification of "issues" or problems from a reading to real–life represents a transfer of information from abstract to reality and some children may find this difficult. This also allows you to metacognitively model, carefully choosing problems that are easier to spot and apply. The use of *Time for Kids* or *Scholastic News* will typically portray issues that are more child friendly than what may be found in your local newspaper. Kids could rank the "issues" based upon the evidence that teams present. If they created an "action plan for community change," thinking will shine.

In this lesson young students are challenged to distinguish fiction from reality, build empathy, and try to solve a real-world problem. This may only occur at a rudimentary level, but the exercise of identifying real issues and finding solutions is a valuable one. Students will use fiction to compel them to apply themes to the real-world. Learners will experience thinking modeled by their peers and the collective minds of a group will produce a better solution than individually.

| Lesson: | Wacky World Problems—Third or Fourth grade (a 3–4 session unit) |
|---|---|
| Learning Targets: | Students will use credible databases to investigate answers<br>Students will speak using vocabulary of the research discipline<br>Students will practice speaking with text-based answers |
| Essential Questions | What are some real-world issues needing solutions?<br>How can we assess real-world issues?<br>Can we brainstorm possible solutions? |
| Guiding Questions | How can we use a credible database to investigate answers?<br>Can we use evidence and data to support a position? |

| Text | Fiction: Dave Pilkey's *DOGZILLA* (or *KatKong*) |
|---|---|
| | Nonfiction: Local Newspapers, Time for Kids, Scholastic News , NewsELA.com, or other equivalent databases such as: |
| | KidsInfoBit <www.gale.cengage.com/**InfoBits**> |
| | EBSCO Primary Search <http://www.ebscohost.com/us-elementary-schools/primary-search> |
| | eLibrary <http://www.elibrary.com> |
| | and other nonfiction sources suitable for grade 3-5 |

| Power words | irresistible, annual, canine, crater, depths, mysterious, residents, colossal, residents, terrifying, creature, ancient, extremely, dreadful, commanding, prehistoric, assemble, tremendous, muster, horrify, confident, community |
|---|---|
| | See sample "Quiz-Quiz-Trade" game cards at the end of this lesson. |

| Vocabulary of library discipline | Keywords, evidence, investigate, claim, source, credible, support |
|---|---|

| CCSS Objectives | x | Vocabulary use | x | Solve real-world issues | x | Discuss, interpret, explain, debate, |
|---|---|---|---|---|---|---|
| | x | Nonfiction use | x | Research | x | Use formal English |
| | x | Close reading | x | Build and present knowledge | x | Rigor |
| | x | Evidence-Based Claim | x | Investigate | x | Relevance |

| Rigor | This Pilkey book is not a very tough read. In fact, it does not take focus or sustained attention to get to the end of this anemic literary gem. The Lexile, readability measure, comes in at a 720, which is just perfect, however, for your late elementary students. With only a few sentences on a page, we really can't call this rigorous by Common Core standards. The vocabulary is what saves this book, for your justification as material used in instruction. The vocabulary is so rich that is trumps the lack of rigor. Most read aloud books should be used with an activity (task as in "reader and the task") which requires the kids to think. |
|---|---|
| | Define the vocabulary words ahead of time and play a vocabulary game after the read such as quiz-quiz trade or Vocabulary Bingo. See the bookmark below, and send copies home inside your students' weekly checkout books. "Cool words to make you sound smart." When you send home a bookmark, you are sending a message home to parents and caregivers that their children are "learning" in the library. |

| Relevance | It would be a far reaching claim that we could use this text to solve a real-world problem, as the CCSS encourages us to have students do. Even though the reader is asked at the end of the book . . .*how to save the town*, this is not the type of problem that the CCSS expects our students to spend a great deal of time contemplating. Genies, dragons, gargoyles, Neptune, megalodon, and other mythical beasts are just a few other terrifying creatures that have captured literary attention many times over, but don't qualify for "real-world problems" that need to be solved. However, we could use this book as a *hook to have these third graders brainstorm what we are, or should be afraid of—or need to solve.* |
|---|---|

| Reader and the task | After reading the Pilkey book and completing the academic vocabulary word games, the students are ready for some "real-world" connection. Listed below are a few investigations that have been field tested.<br><br>EQ: What are some real-world problems or issues that need to be solved?<br><br>• Pre-choose some newspapers, or print various articles out of newspapers, Time for Kids, NewsELA.com or other sources which have concrete "issues" within the article that students could "grasp." In field-testing, students using general local papers to identify real-world problems, did not make efficient use of time as those classes whose librarian pre-chose 10 newspaper articles which were cognitively appropriate.<br>• Working collaboratively in groups, have the children scan and read newspapers for "real" problems or issues and contribute those to a graffiti wall. During this endeavor, you will likely be asked the meanings of words they read and you could practice decoding and finding meaning by surrounding words. You could practice "vocabulary flooding" (synonyms) when they ask you. You could have another graffiti wall of "new words in the neighborhood" which they could fill up as they read. The reading endeavor will likely be a close reading activity as you have given them a "reason to read."<br>• Have the third graders choose a topic from their real-world problem wall to investigate— either individually or as a group. Tell them they will be investigators and will need to dig deeply to find out about an issue and make a "claim." Their claim will be what to do about the issue. High School students would have no problem with this. However, elementary students may need some guidance or some pre-chosen texts to examine. In fact, you could even choose primary source texts from the 1800s (or another period they are studying) and ask them to examine what the real problems were of the time.<br>• This research endeavor could lead to nonfiction reading (CCSS objectives) and text-based answers (CCSS objectives). |
|---|---|
| Assessment | Student self-assessment bookmarks are recommended. Students would use these as a guide for finishing the task as well as insuring that the expectations are met. Expectations for an exemplary knowledge product are listed and checked off.<br>See example below.<br><br>Graphic organizers will be helpful to build an evidence-based claim, with students finding "evidence" that their issue is real. What data can they produce? Why did they choose this issue?<br><br>Graphic organizers will also help them brainstorm solutions. This is the essence of "solving real-world issues." |
| Think Tank Spotlight | Although this lesson starts off in a passive mode, the reader has been set up to be an active listener for vocabulary. Student-centered vocabulary games hit the lower end of Bloom Taxonomy. However, those activities are a pre-cursor and hook to compel the students to compare and contrast fiction "problems" to real-world life. When the students "identify" problems they are half-way up Bloom's and by the end of this lesson, learners have created an evidence-based claim and are ready to argue for their real-world problem. Problem-solving is all the way up Bloom's and generates expert thinkers.<br><br>As they plead for those in power to address their issue, they have reached the top of Blooms and beyond. |

| Blooms Barometer | Remembering | Understanding | Applying | Analyzing | Evaluating | Creating |
|---|---|---|---|---|---|---|
| | x | x | x | x | x | x |

From *Think Tank Library: Brain-Based Learning Plans for New Standards, Grades K–5* by Paige Jaeger and Mary Boyd Ratzer. Santa Barbara, CA: Libraries Unlimited. Copyright © 2015.

| Standards Spotlight | **Common Core**<br>• Speaking and Listening Standards: Discuss, interpret, explain, present claims and findings, use formal English<br>• Research to build and present knowledge<br>• Use formal English<br>  [© Copyright 2010. National Governors Association Center for Best Practices and Council of Chief State School Officers. All rights reserved.]<br><br>**C3 Social Studies:**<br>• Civics: Participation and Deliberation: Applying Civic Virtues and Democratic Principles<br>• Global Interconnections<br>• Liberty, Economics, and other frameworks |
|---|---|

### Sample Vocabulary Game
### Directions for Quiz-Quiz Trade:

- Create vocabulary cards (1 for everyone) with a power word on one side and definition on the opposite side.
- Each child starts with a card and "quizzes" another student on the meaning. *"Do you know what Colossal means?"* The partner is looking at the word and the student has to describe it using the words on the back (meaning).
- The other child then quizzes the partner on his word—perhaps uses it in a sentence, etc.
- Students exchange cards and then go quiz someone else.
- This continues until all words have been used and traded.

### *Student self-assessment checklist:*

| Task Accomplished | Task |
|---|---|
| | We can identify real-world problems and explain why we consider these important |
| | We can identify keywords for investigating our real-world problem |
| | We can find credible information on my team's chosen problem |
| | We can assess whether my information in credible, accurate, and usable |
| | We have embedded at least 5 power words into our claim from this list: irresistible, annual, canine, crater, depths, mysterious, residents, colossal, residents, terrifying, creature, ancient (more from your list . . . ) |
| | We are ready to discuss our real-world problem with the class and have used evidence to support our claim. |
| | We ready to argue why this problem needs to be addressed by people in power and are ready to suggest solutions. |

Quiz – Quiz – Trade sample cards:

| | |
|---|---|
| colossal | terrify |
| ancient | crater |
| residents | annual |
| irresistible | mysterious |

| | |
|---|---|
| frighten<br>scare<br>afraid<br>terrify | huge<br>giant<br>gigantic<br>enormous<br>colossal |
| ground cavity<br>deep cavern<br>deep hole in the ground | archaic<br>very old<br>ages-old<br>over 1,000 years old<br>antique |
| happens every year<br>once a year | people who live in [a house]<br>neighbors<br>inhabitants |
| must-have<br>mouth-watering<br>alluring<br>enticing<br>tempting | strange<br>unexplained<br>unsolved<br>baffling<br>peculiar |

**Our real-world problem needing an action plan for change is:**

_____

_____

_____

**Reason:**



**Evidence from a credible source:**



**Information from a credible source:**



**Data from a credible source:**



**Team recommendations for change or concern:**

# Decoding Difficult Words and Dialogic Read Alouds          Grades 3–4

## WHAT IS THE BIG IDEA?

The Common Core asks us to embrace "literacy across the disciplines" and to purposefully embrace vocabulary. Vocabulary is a key to comprehension and that is why this lesson has been included. Words build comprehension and comprehension builds deep understanding. A library time should move beyond simple read alouds to what is now called, dialogic reading.

Dialogic Reading is *dialoging within the text and outside of the text, while reading the text*. It is not meant to interrupt fluency, but amend the experience to metacognitively model higher level thought and essential comprehension skills. Kids who cannot think will learn how to think by seeing thinking modeled for them. This simple poem lesson is included to serve as an example of how a teacher-librarian can: model fluency, model decoding of difficult words, and have a dialogic discussion during a read aloud.

A two-voice poem from one of Mary Ann Hoberman's *You Read to Me and I'll Read to You* books provides a perfect example for this. Using this short two-voice, two-page poem provides an opportunity to dialogically demonstrate what we would do when we don't know a word. We can equip the students with steps to decoding. There are 11 academic vocabulary words in this poem, adding to the child's comprehension toolbox. As a teacher-librarian, you should model the correct pronunciation prior to reading this poem and ask the students to repeat after you. In addition, you can point out how to decipher meaning, when they do not know a word: Look in the neighborhood for clues. Do they feel it is a positive or a negative word? Is there a synonym close by? Is there a clue close-by? Equip the students with three simple steps:

1. See any Synonyms?
2. Look for who's in the neighborhood?
3. Are the neighbors positive or negative?

Consider packaging this decoding approach as a possible acronym such as SLIP **S**ynonyms? **L**ook for **I**nteresting clues? **P**ositive or negative connotation?) Acronyms are mnemonic devices that help students remember things. They are thinking tricks. In this case it will help students remember just what to do when they see a word they do not know.

In this lesson we can also examine the content and create an evidence-based claim answering the question, "Who was smarter: The dragon or the knight?" This simple question provides the "purpose" to closely read for details. Without a reason to read, students lose the stamina and fortitude to continue. This open-ended question, however silly, will frame a close reading experience. In closely reading, they will likely trip over the new vocabulary and read them a few times as they try to figure out their answer and support it with textual evidence. In addition, we can embrace our own library standards by asking a simple keyword searching question on our handout.

If your students are enjoying this poem, you may wish to consider going beyond the learning goals of decoding and embrace the speaking and listening standards of the Common Core by asking them to perform this with a partner.

This poem provides an opportunity to teach the valuable decoding skills which will link to comprehension and understanding. We cannot over emphasize that we want our students to be equipped with strategies to increase their abilities. A teacher may wish to accompany this lesson with a dictionary endeavor. Remember: Dictionary and skill is not the focus. Building brains through increased vocabulary and comprehension is vital.

This example shows in-text application opportunities for decoding. The words circled show connections to each other or to "clues" for decoding. This models how to use this short poem to teach a valuable comprehension skill.

"You're not very well behaved.

Remember that young girl I saved?"

"You mean that damsel in distress?

You rescued her, I guess."

From: Hoberman, Mary Ann, and Michael Emberley. *You read to me, I'll read to you: very short scary tales to read together.* New York NY.: Little, Brown and Co., 2007. Print.

| Lesson: | Decoding Difficult Words Grade 3–4 | | | | | | |
|---|---|---|---|---|---|---|---|
| Learning Targets: | Students will closely read and make an evidence-based claim<br>Students will learn skills to decode difficult words<br>Students will practice speaking with text-based answers and decoding difficult words | | | | | | |
| Essential Questions: | What can we do when we don't know a word?<br>What tools can I use to discover the meaning of words?<br>Who was smarter the dragon or the knight? | | | | | | |
| Text | Nonfiction: *You Read to Me, I'll Read to You: Very Short Scary Tales to Read Together.* Hoberman, Mary Ann, and Michael Emberley. | | | | | | |
| Power words | Knight, Gnaw, Armor, Aflame, Expire, Distress, Damsel, Distressing, Rescue, Noble, Deed | | | | | | |
| Vocabulary of library discipline | Keywords, evidence, claim, comprehend | | | | | | |
| CCSS Objectives | x | Vocabulary use | x | Solve real-world issues | x | Discuss, interpret, explain, debate, | |
| | x | Nonfiction use | | Research | x | Use formal English | |
| | x | Close reading | | Build and present knowledge | x | Rigor | |
| | x | Evidence-Based Claim | | Investigate | x | Relevance | |
| Rigor | This book is written by a poet-laureate and exemplifies a fun, challenging poem which does not talk-down to the reader. It is a perfect example for modeling decoding of difficult words. Pronounce the vocabulary words ahead of time and share with the students that building vocabulary builds brains and comprehension. This skill, therefore, is an imperative skill to share with students equipping them to discover new words. | | | | | | |

| Relevance | There are no dragons or knights in our world—that we know of. Therefore, it is a hard claim to connect relevance. However, the skill is relevant to our lives and we can start the conversation by asking students, "What do you do when you come across a difficult word?" How can we build our brains in a way similar to the way knight practices his art of defense? |
|---|---|
| Reader and the task | EQ: Who was smarter: The dragon or the knight?<br>EQ: What do you do when you encounter difficult words?<br>Model the decoding strategy of decoding and deciphering meaning: S-L-I-P<br>1. Sound like another word. . . . or part of another word?<br>2. Is the "sound" in the sentence—Positive or negative? (connotation)<br>3. Neighborhood words?—Are there other words close by giving us a hint? |
| Assessment | Did the student support their claim with evidence from the text?<br>Can the students use the power words within their writing and speaking?<br>Can the students successfully decode the power words using the SLIP suggestions? |
| Think Tank Spotlight | Although this lesson starts off in a passive mode, the reader has been set up to be an active listener for vocabulary. Student-centered vocabulary activity hits halfway up Bloom's Taxonomy, but provides a necessary skill and tool to use henceforth.<br><br>Vocabulary is the key to comprehension and deep learning. That is why we have included this lesson<br><br>By asking students to think about the poem's characters and their actions, we are asking the students to closely read for details and be able to defend a position. This is an evidence-based argument. |

| Blooms Barometer | Remembering<br>x | Understanding<br>x | Applying<br>x | Analyzing<br>x | Evaluating<br>x | Creating<br>x |
|---|---|---|---|---|---|---|

| Standards Spotlight | **Common Core**<br>• Speaking and Listening Standards: Discuss, interpret, explain, present claims and findings, use formal English<br>• Research to build and present knowledge<br>• Use formal English<br>• Refer to details and examples in a text when explaining what the text says explicitly and when drawing inferences from the text<br>• Describe . . . Drawing on specific details in the text (e.g., a character's thoughts, words, or actions)<br><br>[© Copyright 2010. National Governors Association Center for Best Practices and Council of Chief State School Officers. All rights reserved.] |
|---|---|

## The Dragon and the Knight
*You Read to Me, I'll Read to You*: by Mary Ann Hoberman

**Cool words make you sound smart: I can identify keywords to search the catalog. If I don't know a word, I can SLIP** (Sounds Like—is it Positive or Negative?)

**With your group, create a claim:** *Who was smarter: the dragon or the knight?*

| | |
|---|---|
| **Who was smarter?** | |
| **Evidence 1** | |
| **Evidence 2** | |

| If you wanted to find more information on this topic, what KEYWORDS would you use in the OPAC? | I know these impressive words: |
|---|---|
| _____ | _____Knight |
| _____ | _____Gnaw |
| _____ | _____Armor |
| | _____Aflame |
| | _____Expire |
| | _____Distress |
| | _____Damsel |
| | _____Distressing |
| | _____Rescue |
| | _____Noble |
| | _____Deed |

# Mythbusters                                          3rd–4th Grade Research Unit

This innovative lesson idea was submitted by local librarian, Susan Kirby-Lemon, Librarian for Skano Elementary School in Clifton Park. She and a third grade teacher, never underestimates the abilities of their students. By tapping into natural curiosity and a popular television show, this lesson uses multiple texts and connects ERLA and science. Theme and variations to this lesson may be found online, but listed below is a unique text-set to accompany this.

Students pose as scientists who understand that there are natural processes occurring on earth. These include everyday events, such as the water cycle and energy from the sun; and extreme events, such as floods, and volcanic eruptions. Students also have read books which tell how ancient people tried to explain these natural processes through stories, or myths. They are set up as mythbusters who will travel back in time to teach the ancient *gurus* the real natural science tied to their myths.

When learners explain the science of natural processes in their own 21st century words, and apply the realization that science can be proven while myths cannot, they demonstrate understanding beyond factual recall. The scientific thinking in this lesson weaves together information literacy in the following ways:

- Exploring and accessing information
- Analyzing information
- Evaluating information
- Organizing information
- Constructing meaning from information
- Drawing conclusions substantiated by data or facts, developing hypotheses
- Communicating information

| Lesson: | Mythbusters! |
|---|---|
| **Learning Targets:** | Students will:<br>Read and determine main idea and supporting details<br>Research science and apply it to real-world situations<br>Investigate, synthesize, conclude, and explain<br>Think like a scientist<br>Work as a part of a team to explore and analyze scientific cause and effect<br>draw scientific conclusions, With guidance<br>Compare and contrast |
| **Essential Questions:** | How can scientific investigation uncover scientific truth?<br>How has science helped us to understand the world around us?<br>Are their questions which science cannot explain? |
| **Research Text** | Pebble Go database (PebbleGo.com), Nonfiction books, encyclopedias, periodical articles at an appropriate reading levels for the grade level. Scaffold article difficulty accommodating differentiated instruction where necessary. |

|  | **MYTH** | | **SCIENCE** |
|---|---|---|---|
| **Myth Text Set** (Or, others in your collection) | *The Battle of the Olympians and the Titans (Greek Myths)*, by Cari Meister | | Earthquakes, lightning, thunder |
| | *Ye Ho Waah: Cherokee Origin Myth* http://nativeamericans.mrdonn.org/stories/myth/cherokee.html | | Erosion |
| | *Children's Dictionary of Mythology: Incan Flood*, A Franklin Watts library. (book) | | Flood |
| | *Ancient Egypt: Tales of Gods and Pharaohs*, by Marcia Williams (book) | | Sun's power, day and night, hurricanes, floods, drought |
| | *The Voyages of Odysseus*, by Lynne Weiss (book) | | Storms at sea |
| | *Zeus: King of the Gods, God of Sky and Storms*, by Teri Temple. (book) | | Thunder & lightning, volcanoes |
| | Mythological creatures: a classical bestiary: tales of strange being, fabulous creatures, fearsome beasts, and hideous monsters from ancient Greek mythology, by Lynn Curlee. (book) | | Earthquakes, hurricanes |
| | *Master Man: A Tall Tale of Nigeria* by Aaron Shepard. *(book)* | | Thunder and lightning |
| | *D'Aulaires Book of Norse Myths*, by Edgar Parin D'Aulaire. *(book)* | | Wind & storms, plants growing, wind & rain |
| | *Poseidon: God of the Sea and Earthquakes* by Teri Temple. *Child's World. 2014.* | | Earthquakes, storms, whirlpools |
| **Power words** | Varies with myth chosen ask students to create their own person word wall or word bank and contribute to a vocabulary graffiti wall or bulletin board | | |
| **Vocabulary of library discipline** | Analyze, investigate, evidence, interpret data, use details to understand concepts, categorize facts and observations, draw conclusions from evidence | | |

| **CCSS Objectives Observable in Students** | x | Vocabulary use | x | Solve real-world issues | x | Discuss, interpret, explain |
|---|---|---|---|---|---|---|
| | x | Nonfiction use | x | Research | | Use formal English |
| | x | Close reading | x | Build and present knowledge | x | Rigor |
| | | Evidence-Based Claim | | | x | Relevance |

From *Think Tank Library: Brain-Based Learning Plans for New Standards, Grades K–5* by Paige Jaeger and Mary Boyd Ratzer. Santa Barbara, CA: Libraries Unlimited. Copyright © 2015.

| | |
|---|---|
| **Rigor** | Use the scientific language of the discipline<br>Collaboratively investigate and recording data from a transect in a forest<br>Read nonfiction texts closely to understand scientific concepts<br>Distinguish the ecology of two types of forests by informed observation<br>Think scientifically<br>Communicate and share data to draw conclusions<br>Use exact measurement in setting up a transect<br>Construct meaning from direct experience in combination with background knowledge<br>Comprehend the idea that explanations for the natural world in the past were based on imaginative or speculative notions that were not supported by scientific evidence<br>Comprehend that even now without scientific proof unproven ideas are just myths |
| **Relevance** | Science comes to life when it is applied in real-world scenarios. This lesson gives students the opportunity to investigate, synthesize, conclude and share their knowledge in a self-directed full-of-choice assignment. Students are given the opportunity to voice their own conclusions and creations. Students are mentored by teacher-scientists and can post their creations on-line, virtually, using Smore.com, a wiki, a class Mythbusters blog, and more. Students collaborate to analyze and think like a scientist. |
| **Reader and the task** | • Students choose partners and read through a text set- minimum of six.<br>• Students determine what the ancients were trying to explain in one of the myths (how something was created, where something comes from, etc.).<br>• Students will chart how the myth describes the occurrence and investigate the science behind it.<br>• Students create a visual aid to support your knowledge.<br>• Students teach a "lesson" to the ancients.<br>• Students reading nonfiction scientific texts will develop conceptual knowledge science as applied to the natural world. |
| **Assessment** | Students use a checklist that informs expectations and guides investigation. Students develop a scientific Infographic, or picture of the science behind the myth.<br>Completing the Show Me the Science graphic organizer to gather evidence. Students successfully convey mythbusting to ancients and are able to articulate "science" using the vocabulary of the discipline for their topic (erosion: time, land, surface, cause and effect, sea cliff, hillside, etc.). |
| **Think Tank Spotlight** | Students<br>• Expand knowledge while seeking meaning.<br>• Communicate and share subject area expertise Reasoning is increasingly based on supporting facts and details.<br>• Develop self-awareness about thinking and learning.<br>• Understand and manipulate multiple causes and effects.<br>• Discern change over time Applying science to real life scenarios.<br>• Use fact to solve fiction.<br>• Reason abstractly. |

| Blooms Barometer | Remembering x | Understanding x | Applying x | Analyzing x | Evaluating x | Creating x |
|---|---|---|---|---|---|---|

| Standards Spotlight | **Common Core**<br>• Use precise language and domain-specific vocabulary to inform about or explain the topic.<br>• Refer to details and examples in a text when explaining what the text says explicitly and when drawing inferences from the text.<br>• Draw evidence from literary or informational texts to support analysis, reflection, and research.<br>• Explain events, procedures, ideas, or concepts in a historical, scientific, or technical text, including what happened and why, based on specific information in the text.<br>• Interpret information presented visually, orally, or quantitatively (e.g., in charts, graphs, diagrams, time lines, animations, or interactive elements on Web pages) and explain how the information contributes to an understanding of the text in which it appears.<br>• Integrate information from two texts on the same topic to write or speak about the subject knowledgeably.<br>• Draw points, lines, line segments, rays, angles (right, acute, obtuse).<br>[© Copyright 2010. National Governors Association Center for Best Practices and Council of Chief State School Officers. All rights reserved.]<br><br>**Mathematics**<br>• Represent and interpret data<br>• Reason abstractly and quantitatively<br>• Model with mathematics<br>[© Copyright 2010. National Governors Association Center for Best Practices and Council of Chief State School Officers. All rights reserved.]<br><br>**Next Generation Science Standards – Science and Engineering Practices**<br>• **Developing and Using Model** – Develop a model to describe phenomena<br>• **Earth Materials and Systems** – Rainfall helps to shape the land and affects the types of living things found in a region. Water, ice, wind, living organisms, and gravity break rocks, soils, and sediments into smaller particles and move them around.<br>• **Plate Tectonics and Large-Scale System Interactions** The locations of mountain ranges, deep ocean trenches, ocean floor structures, earthquakes, and volcanoes occur in patterns. Most earthquakes and volcanoes occur in bands that are often along the boundaries between continents and oceans. Major mountain chains form inside continents or near their edges.<br><br>Copyright 2013 Achieve, Inc. All rights reserved |

*Mythbusters—Show them the science!*

| | |
|---|---|
| **What happened in the myth?** | |
| **Why did the ancients say it happened?** | |
| **Cause in myth:** | |
| **Effect in myth:** | |
| **Possible science topics to look up:** | |
| **Keywords for searching** | |
| **Science says:** | |
| **Science says:** | |
| **Science says:** | |
| **Explanation in my own words:** | |

Team Members:

_____

## Myth and Research Notes

**Part 1: Make a Decision**

Title of myth chosen (from those you have read):

_____

Natural process you will "bust" (choose only one)

_____

How the myth explains the natural process:
Be certain to use evidence directly from the text to support how the ancients explained it):

From *Think Tank Library: Brain-Based Learning Plans for New Standards, Grades K–5* by Paige Jaeger and Mary Boyd Ratzer. Santa Barbara, CA: Libraries Unlimited. Copyright © 2015.

**Part 2: Research the Natural Process**

Using the resources available, research your topic to gain an understanding of how it really happens. Take notes in the box below using bullets and and paraphrasing. Take at least three notes while you research.

How does science explain its occurrence?

From *Think Tank Library: Brain-Based Learning Plans for New Standards, Grades K–5* by Paige Jaeger and Mary Boyd Ratzer. Santa Barbara, CA: Libraries Unlimited. Copyright © 2015.

Myth Busters – Script Story Organizer
Names:

| | Describe your picture here | Script |
|---|---|---|
| Picture 1: Title slide | | |
| Picture 2: Ancients Say | | |
| Picture 3: Science Says | | |

From *Think Tank Library: Brain-Based Learning Plans for New Standards, Grades K–5* by Paige Jaeger and
Mary Boyd Ratzer. Santa Barbara, CA: Libraries Unlimited. Copyright © 2015.

# Ecology of Deciduous and Coniferous Forests    Grade 4

## WHAT'S THE BIG IDEA?

A fourth grade class in Berne Know Westerlo Elementary School, New York, ventured into a local forest preserve to gather data on living things and their habitats. They were prepared to think like scientists by observing things and classifying them into: producers, consumers, and decomposers. This was far from rote learning. It was the essence of student-engagement and real-world experience. It is Inquiry at its best. That is why this lesson from Agnes Zeller has been included as a Think Tank example.

In collaboration with a local forest preserve scientist, teachers began to build background knowledge on biotic and abiotic elements of an ecosystem and add ecology vocabulary to the class word wall. Students honed math skills, vocabulary, and investigation techniques. Preparing for a day in a forest where they will gather data on living things and habitats, students learn about three types of organisms in northern deciduous and coniferous forests. They learn about the roles organisms play, and how they are dependent on obtaining energy and how they interact with other organisms. Students in class practice setting up a five meter by five meter transect, which is their grid for organism data gathering. They practice measuring their transect with rope, as well as investigating and recording data on prepared data sheets.

Various close reading text assignments build a foundation of understanding and vocabulary. Information investigations happen in the library using the PebbleGo database and other resources to build factual and conceptual knowledge through. This new knowledge is applied during the real-world experience in the forest.

Field trip day arrives and collaborative teams of energetic young scientists, who will model scientific thinking, arrive at the forest. They are guided by forest preserve biologists in their data gathering in deciduous and coniferous forests.

Data and observations are charted, shared, analyzed, and extrapolated to draw conclusions about the 22,000 acre preserve in relation to the area of the transects explored by the class. Changes in the forest over time, strategies to sustain the forests, and competition between species are discussed. This is scientific thinking. This is mathematics, applied.

You can replicate this experience for your budding scientists by partnering with Environmental organizations in your area.

| Lesson: | Ecology of Deciduous and Coniferous Forests Grade–4 |
|---|---|
| Learning Targets: | Use the vocabulary of forest ecology knowingly<br>Read and view informational resources at the appropriate Lexile to understand scientific concepts in the domain of forest ecology<br>Develop skills in data gathering and charting quantitative information<br>Work as a part of a team to explore and analyze life forms in a forest<br>With guidance extrapolate data to draw scientific conclusions<br>Compare and contrast deciduous and coniferous forests |
| Essential Questions: | How do organisms have different and interdependent roles in the ecology of a deciduous and coniferous forest?<br>How can scientific investigation and data gathering uncover scientific truth? |
| Text | Databases, nonfiction books, nonfiction eBooks, encyclopedias, periodical articles at appropriate reading levels, etc. |
| Power words | deciduous, coniferous, organism, decomposer, producer, consumer, carnivore, omnivore, ecology, transect, competition, preserve, invasive, habitats |

| Vocabulary of library discipline | Analyze, investigate, record data, interpret data, use details to understand concepts, categorize facts and observations, draw conclusions from data | | | | | |
|---|---|---|---|---|---|---|
| **CCSS Goals** | x | Vocabulary use | x | Solve real-world issues | x | Discuss, interpret, explain |
| | x | Nonfiction use | x | Research | | Use formal English |
| | x | Close reading | x | Build and present knowledge | x | Rigor |
| | | Evidence-Based Claim | | | x | Relevance |

| **Rigor** | Use the scientific language of the discipline.<br>Collaboratively investigate and recording data from a transect in a forest.<br>Read nonfiction texts closely to understand scientific concepts.<br>Distinguish the ecology of two types of forests by informed observation.<br>Think scientifically.<br>Communicate and share data to draw conclusions.<br>Use exact measurement in setting up transect.<br>Construct meaning from direct experience in combination with background knowledge. |
|---|---|
| **Relevance** | The setting for the forest ecology learning experience is very local and immediate.<br>Students in teams look closely at organisms previously overlooked, discovering the life around them.<br>Students are mentored by scientists from the local forest preserve, and accompanied on the field trip by parent volunteers.<br>Students collaborate to record accurate data, and develop original questions.<br>Experts in forest ecology guide learners in their observation, analysis, and extrapolation. |
| **Reader and the task** | Students read nonfiction scientific texts and will develop conceptual knowledge of living organisms in deciduous and coniferous forests, identify them, and prepare for the field experience by determining where and how they live. |
| **Assessment** | Guided practice with a checklist that informs expectations and a plan for investigation.<br>Concept map to analyze facts and concepts from research.<br>Reflection and feedback from peers.<br>Use of a graphic organizer to gather evidence include a graphic organizer to gather evidence.<br>Rubric for the extended learning experience in the form of a scientific field journal. |
| **Think Tank spotlight** | • Expanding knowledge creates a platform for meaning with new information.<br>• Acquiring new knowledge is easier when subject area expertise increases.<br>• Reasoning is increasingly based on supporting facts and details.<br>• Developing self-awareness about thinking and learning is boosted.<br>• Writing and communicating increases focus of performance in complex tasks.<br>• Planning and goal setting evolve from amateur to apprentice.<br>• Creating questions move from a groundwork of facts to HOW, WHY, SHOULD, WHAT IF.<br>• Understanding about multiple causes and multiple effects is exercised.<br>• Discerning change over time can be understood and represented. |

| | • Recognizing relationships among patterns and processes is easier.<br>• Integrating information from sources is increasingly based on evaluation of that information.<br>• Linking ideas within and across categories employs language that makes distinctions.<br>• Reasoning abstractly and quantitatively moves beyond concrete thinking use parallel construction. | | | | | |
|---|---|---|---|---|---|---|
| **Blooms Barometer** | Remembering<br>x | Understanding<br>x | Applying<br>x | Analyzing<br>x | Evaluating<br>x | Creating<br>x |

| | |
|---|---|
| **Standards Spotlight** | **Common Core Standards:**<br>**ELA**<br>• Use precise language and domain-specific vocabulary to inform about or explain the topic.<br>• Refer to details and examples in a text when explaining what the text says explicitly and when drawing inferences from the text.<br>• Draw evidence from literary or informational texts to support analysis, reflection, and research.<br>• Explain events, procedures, ideas, or concepts in a historical, scientific, or technical text, including what happened and why, based on specific information in the text.<br>• Interpret information presented visually, orally, or quantitatively (e.g., in charts, graphs, diagrams, time lines, animations, or interactive elements on Web pages) and explain how the information contributes to an understanding of the text in which it appears.<br>• Integrate information from two texts on the same topic to write or speak about the subject knowledgeably.<br>• Draw points, lines, line segments, rays, angles (right, acute, obtuse), and perpendicular and parallel lines. Identify these in two-dimensional figure<br>• Draw on information from multiple print or digital sources, demonstrating the ability to locate an answer to a question quickly or to solve a problem efficiently.<br><br>**Mathematics**<br>• Represent and interpret data<br>• Reason abstractly and quantitatively<br>• Model with mathematics<br><br>[© Copyright 2010. National Governors Association Center for Best Practices and Council of Chief State School Officers. All rights reserved.]<br><br>**Next Generation Science Standards:**<br>**Disciplinary Core Ideas**<br>• **Interdependent Relationships in Ecosystems**<br>The food of almost any kind of animal can be traced back to plants. Organisms are related in food webs in which some animals eat plants for food and other animals eat the animals that eat plants. Some organisms, such as fungi and bacteria, break down dead organisms (both plants or plants parts and animals) and therefore operate as "decomposers." Decomposition eventually restores (recycles) some materials back to the soil. Organisms can survive only in environments in which their particular needs are met. A healthy ecosystem is one in which multiple species of different types are each able to meet their needs in a relatively stable web of life. Newly introduced species can damage the balance of an ecosystem.<br><br>**Science and Engineering Practices**<br>• Develop a model to describe phenomenon<br>• Copyright 2013 Achieve, Inc. All rights reserved |

**Thinking about Evidence**

## My Conclusion

_____
_____
_____
_____

### Evidence

_____
_____
_____

### Evidence

_____
_____
_____

### Evidence

_____
_____
_____

### Evidence

_____
_____
_____

**How did I evaluate my evidence? Is my evidence FACT?**

**Field Data Sheet Collection Tool**
**Energy Flow in the Forest**

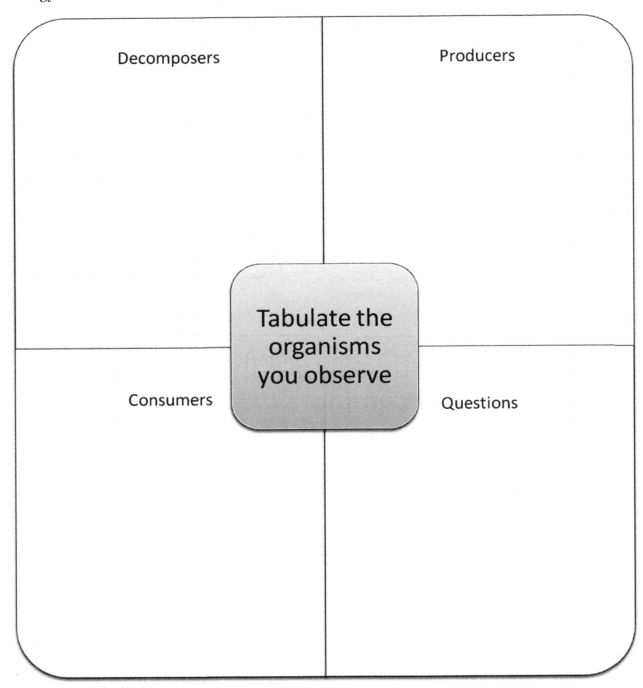

# State Report Makeover: E pluribus Unum!          Grades 4–5

## WHAT IS THE BIG IDEA?

All around the United States students are writing low-level state reports in epidemic proportions, merely transferring simple unimportant factoids such as state birds or state insects. These reports which have been successfully written for decades fall short of rigor, higher-level thought and the Common Core bar of solving real-world problems.

Inserting a few essential questions focusing on the "enduring understanding" will easily transform these reports into learning endeavors requiring students to think and conclude about the role their state plays in "creating a more perfect union." The Understanding by Design (UBD) theory would ask the teacher to contemplate, what is it that you really want your students to take-away at the end of the unit? That there is a big amusement park in Ohio? Or, that Ohio demarks the edge of the "megalopolis" and the beginning of the "breadbasket"? Which take-away has more value?

In the Constitution's Preamble, we are confronted with our founding fathers' intentions: *"We the People of the United States, in Order to form a more perfect Union, establish Justice, insure domestic Tranquility, provide for the common defense, promote the general Welfare, and secure the Blessings of Liberty to ourselves and our Posterity, do ordain and establish this Constitution for the United States of America."* That is a primary source document that could be introduced at the beginning of this unit.

Our currency includes the phrase, *E pluribus Unum,* Out of many, one. That is the enduring understanding that we as educators should be striving for our students to understand. Your instruction will be filled with rigor and success, if your students can answer the essential question: *How does your state contribute to the Preamble of our Constitution and our nation's motto, E pluribus Unum.* That is instruction aligned with the Common Core, the national Social Studies Standards, and the gold standard of UBD. and UDL.

By hooking our students into examining coins at the very beginning, you are starting this project off with your major motto: E pluribus Unum. In the pockets of their pants, they are likely to hold the key to this state report endeavor.

Your students can still research their choice of states, and examine similar facts as they have in the past, but this time it will be done through a different, new critical lens. In this lesson, we have even used the lens visually to teach the students a premise of good research perspective. The enduring understanding will be something of significance: All for one. One for all.

| Lesson: | E Pluribus Unum! State Report Grades 4–5 |
|---|---|
| **Learning Targets:** | Students will understand the importance of the Preamble and the motto: E Pluribus Unum.<br>Learners will understand how their state, or region, contribute to the welfare of our United States through mutually beneficial and specialized goods and services to meet wants and needs.<br>Learners will link their state's natural resources, climate, topography, and geography to "exports and imports." |
| **Possible Knowledge Product(s)** | • Student's research is synthesized and presented in a "Governor's Convention" The Principal can be invited as the President, and each state governor may have a one minute elevator speech, concisely giving the "State of the State" with key details about how their state contributes to the motto E Pluribus Unum!<br>• The same product could be kicked up a notch with regional governors (students) addressing the President about: regional problems and promise: needs to sustain that region in its important economic role. (For example, how can the water resources of the west sustain agriculture for the good of all?) |

| | |
|---|---|
| | • In addition, students can be asked to create "train cars" for a transcontinental railroad. One car should have "imports" and one car should have "exports" within it, representing what the state, or region, has to offer and needs. Students should color their car to represent their state. The destinations or points of origin of those train cars could be mapped to show how many are indeed one through economic diversity. A state logo or a state slogan could be emblazoned on the train car representing the big idea of that state's contribution. For example: *California feeds America*! Or North Dakota: *An Energy Producer for the Future*, or *Nano Tech Loves New York*!<br>• Possible written products embracing writing standards within the standards could include: Individual State of the State addresses answering the EQ;<br>• A persuasive speech in the Governor's Convention to present evidence to support a claim that the state needs intervention to remain a viable link in the nation's economy<br>• Persuasive Essays: Please Join Us In [state]! |
| **EQs:**<br><br>**Guiding questions:** | How does your state contribute to the welfare of the nation, reflecting the Preamble of our Constitution and our nation's motto, E Pluribus Unum?<br>How does your state or region use its topography, climate, and geography to contribute to the goods and services needed within our union?<br>How did your state use its natural resources, climate, topography, and geography in the past to further the cause of the union?<br>What does your state have to export? Why?<br>What does your state need to import? Why?<br>What are your state's most critical problems and why? (You may want your student's to visit their State Senator's websites to discern issues)<br>What are your state's strengths? Why? |
| **Text** | The Constitution of the United States Preamble, coins and paper currency<br>State books, Grolier online or other encyclopedias such as World Book, current quality periodical articles about the problems, productivity, trade relationships, and economic threats of specific states, other online state resources |
| **Power words** | Please notice how you are weaving together SS, Science, and ELA by embracing vocabulary of more than one discipline. This is the real-world:<br><br>Currency, preamble, constitution, natural resources, government, capital, landmarks, geography, geography, landmarks, biome, habitat, industry, industries, tourist attractions (Caveat—don't major on this! However, let's face it. Some states have *major industries* in their tourist attractions, and this should be the focus—how these contribute to the economy and opportunity of Americans.) |
| **Vocabulary of library discipline** | Analyze, investigate, record data, interpret data, use details to understand concepts, categorize facts and observations, draw conclusions from data, and synthesize |

| CCSS Objectives Observable in Students | | | | | | |
|---|---|---|---|---|---|---|
| | x | Vocabulary use | x | Solve real-world issues | x | Discuss, interpret, explain |
| | x | Nonfiction use | x | Research | x | Use formal English |
| | x | Close reading | x | Build and present knowledge | x | Rigor |
| | x | Evidence-Based Claim | x | Text-Based Answers | x | Relevance |

| | |
|---|---|
| **Rigor** | Using the language of the discipline to explain their state's role in our "union" |
| | Making a real-world connection to a guiding principle of U.S. history |
| | Reading nonfiction texts closely to understand interdependent concepts |
| | Communicating and share data to draw conclusions |
| | Constructing meaning from multiple texts |
| | Representing your state in a *Governor's Convention* |
| | Embracing speaking and listening standards requiring students to contribute to the "State of the State speech." |
| | Constructing an evidence based claim for required action in sustaining economy of states |
| **Relevance** | The relevance of this project connects with a late elementary school student who is given the opportunity to dig into their pocket and connect money to their world. In addition, virtual field trips may be an exciting way to "transport" the learner who may never have the opportunity to leave their "home." |
| | Connecting local areas to favorite sports teams and our inter-connectivity of sports, tourism, and national pride will help to heighten the importance of placing their state into perspective of the whole. |
| **Reader and the task** | Students reading nonfiction materials will start to collect facts to answer the larger question: How do we contribute to the whole. |
| | As texts are read, facts can be recorded based upon "lenses" which help students learn to "categorize" information found. This will later help them synthesize. |
| | Students use facts to form opinions and positions on what their state has to offer and what it needs. Rather than trivial facts such as state birds' students are asked to discover what industries are present and who needs those. This places the facts into context with a national perspective. (If a student can support their opinion with evidence found, then as educators, we give them credit for their success. Not all answers have to fit into a nice box. Some children may end up focusing on agriculture, while others may focus on crime. Each may have data to contribute. |
| | You may choose to place more than one person on a state team, or do this individually based upon time allotments and goals. This is a framework for your locality to modify for local usage |
| **Assessment** | Concept map to analyze facts from research may work well. |
| | Pictorial map of their state or region may help to aid note-taking for natural resources, topography and geography, industries and more evidence-based claims |
| | Elevator speeches presenting knowledge writing of argument |
| | Synthesis of most important facts into controlling big ideas |
| | Use of a graphic organizer to gather evidence sample in text |
| | Written "State of the State" essays should have a rubric (see appendix) sample in text |
| | Students use the vocabulary of the discipline knowingly |
| **Think Tank Spotlight** | Students: |
| | • Expand knowledge creates a platform for meaning and synthesis |
| | • Speak with understanding—not just information |
| | • Reason increasingly based on supporting facts and details |
| | • Develop self-awareness about thinking and learning |
| | • Focus increasingly on "why" and "how is this important" |
| | • Plan and set goals more efficiently |

| | | | | | | |
|---|---|---|---|---|---|---|
| | • Move questions from a groundwork of facts to HOW, WHY, SHOULD, WHAT IF<br>• Understand multiple causes and multiple effects and apply<br>• Discern change over time<br>• Recognize relationships among patterns and processes<br>• Integrate information from sources based on evaluation of that information<br>• Link ideas within and across categories<br>• Makes distinctions<br>• Reason abstractly and quantitatively | | | | | |
| **Blooms Barometer** | Remembering<br>x | Understanding<br>x | Applying<br>x | Analyzing<br>x | Evaluating<br>X | Creating<br>X |

| | |
|---|---|
| **Standards Spotlight** | **Common Core:**<br>**ELA**<br>• Use precise language and domain-specific vocabulary to inform about or explain the topic.<br>• Refer to details and examples in a text when explaining what the text says explicitly and when drawing inferences from the text.<br>• Draw evidence from literary or informational texts to support analysis, reflection, and research.<br>• Explain events, procedures, ideas, or concepts in a historical, scientific, or technical text, including what happened and why, based on specific information in the text.<br>• Interpret information presented visually, orally, or quantitatively (e.g., in charts, graphs, diagrams, time lines, animations, or interactive elements on Web pages) and explain how the information contributes to an understanding of the text in which it appears.<br>• Integrate information from two texts on the same topic to write or speak about the subject knowledgeably.<br>• Draw on information from multiple print or digital sources, demonstrating the ability to locate an answer to a question quickly or to solve a problem efficiently.<br><br>**Mathematics**<br>• Represent and interpret data<br>• Reason abstractly and quantitatively<br><br>**National Science Standards – Disciplinary Core Ideas**<br>• **Interdependent Relationships in Ecosystems**<br>• The food of almost any kind of animal can be traced back to plants. Organisms are related in food webs in which some animals eat plants for food and other animals eat the animals that eat plants. Some organisms, such as fungi and bacteria, break down dead organisms (both plants or plants parts and animals) and therefore operate as "decomposers." Decomposition eventually restores (recycles) some materials back to the soil. Organisms can survive only in environments in which their particular needs are met. A healthy ecosystem is one in which multiple species of different types are each able to meet their needs in a relatively stable web of life. Newly introduced species can damage the balance of an ecosystem. (5-LS2-1)<br>• **Science and Engineering Practices**<br>• **Developing and Using Model** – Develop a model to describe phenomenon<br>Copyright 2013 Achieve, Inc. All rights reserved |

From *Think Tank Library: Brain-Based Learning Plans for New Standards, Grades K–5* by Paige Jaeger and
Mary Boyd Ratzer. Santa Barbara, CA: Libraries Unlimited. Copyright © 2015.

| | Use this handout to focus your investigation. Find important details that a Governor should know |
|---|---|
| **Natural Resources** | |
| **Topography** | |
| **Geography** | |
| **Politics and Government** | |
| **Major Issues** | |
| **Economy and Employment** | |
| **Education** | |
| **Industry** | |

## Country Report Alternatives                    Grades 5–6

## UNITED NATIONS SUMMIT—PROPOSAL FOR INTERNATIONAL AID
## WHAT'S THE BIG IDEA?

From California to the New York Islands country reports are being "done" ubiquitously. Staunchly rooted in the field guide to "Reports Everybody Loves to Hate", this report joins the ranks of bird reports, state reports, animal reports, and biography reports. Most of the time these reports merely transfer facts found on the Internet or within an encyclopedias onto paper or a PowerPoint presentation. Country reports feature factoids such as capitals, rulers, democracies and natural resources that are reported proudly with the absolute assurance that correct answers are filling in every single box. Disaffected learners plow through the task with no hope of meaning or recall, plugging in and going to the next empty box. High flyers get out the glitter and have the thing laminated at the copy store, but have no hope of recall or deep meaning.

While our students are creating "travel brochures" and "fill hypothetical suitcases," other countries are asking their students to examine *mortality rates* and brainstorm solutions for the root causes. The time has come to increase rigor of our country reports and require kids to examine data, think, and solve real-world problems. Low-level country reports can easily be transformed into flat-world experiences, by making global connections to relevant issues that even a young child can understand. By concentrating on the social studies topics of *geography, history, economy, government, culture, science and technology*, students focus not on meaningless "facts" but move to cause and effect, implications of culture and geography, and more.

Brain research demonstrates that teachers can under-estimate the capacity of younger students, and research says in making a lesson harder, a student's brain may be stimulated to investigate and hard-wire new conceptual ideas. When the level of synthesis is reached, new knowledge becomes the building block base for future learning.

In this lesson, we are asking classroom teachers and librarians to begin with an engaging "homework hook" to mine data. This data-mining activity activates thinking and instantly breeds relevance. Students go home and investigate their pantries, refrigerators, dresser drawers, and electronic products for countries of origin. This eye-opening activity brings to light the enduring understanding of "global interdependency." Students return to eagerly map dots and set themselves up for brainstorming "wonder" questions for Inquiry. (If this is not possible, amass 75 such items from your home and school and use those.) From this activity, students wonder, investigate, synthesize, and express (WISE).

After choosing a country that contributes, or fails to contribute, to the global economy, students engage in an investigation of their country, and prepare to represent it as a U.N. ambassador. After students research to discover the promise and perils of their chosen nation, they will need to synthesize this information to speak intelligently as that country's Ambassador.

### Country Report Math and Data Focus:

An embedded piece of this unique **United Nations Summit** incorporates math creating an interdisciplinary learning experience blending ELA, SS, and Math. Extending this lesson to access, select, use, and integrate data and statistics into an evidence-based claim, connects math to the knowledge product and process in many ways.

- The CCSS addresses the use of data in evidence-based claims and arguments. Fact-based decision making starts with math. Understanding the world mathematically is a goal of the CCSS.
- Reading tabular and graphical information and statistics is also a part of the CCSS. Reading complex statistical texts in tabular form introduces comprehension and mathematical understanding.

Rich and authoritative data regarding health, education, environment, and economy is readily available on the Internet and in quality information resources in databases. Data will drive the choice of a problem in a country and a compelling choice for a persuasive essay or evidence based claim presents itself. If malaria is the number one cause of death; if only 12% girls receive an elementary education; if toxins left behind by oil drilling poison the water table; If only 50% of the people are employed, and so on.

To measure a problem, in natural and human terms, also drives decision making and conclusions. Comparative data from country to country spotlights problems needing to be solved. The world can be mapped by infant mortality, malnutrition, drought, unemployment or trade.

**Mathematical Examples:**

**The World Health Organization** (WHO) http://www.who.int/countries/en/ is a searchable and authoritative platform for data related to health. Each country has a detailed breakdown of data related to health. Data and statistics are also displayed comparatively and cumulatively regarding world health. WHO's **Global Health Observatory** portal provides access to data and analyses for monitoring global health. Data is displayed in a number of meaningful ways. Country profiles are comprehensive and detailed. For example, tuberculosis cases can be viewed in a table based on time, and it can be seen where cases are increasing or decreasing. Data can be displayed by income with the input of the Word Bank. Deaths from this disease and countless others are documented. Compelling problems jump off the tables. Links take readers to solutions, informing the learner of ways to solve specific problems.

The World Health Organization website offers data many topics that students should not miss. Be sure to navigate and model accessing:

- Data repository
- World health statistics report
- Statistical reports
- Country statistics
- Map gallery

**Education** – The same broad access and useful information can be found for education through the World Bank Education Stats website: http://data.worldbank.org/topic/education#boxes-box-topic_cust_sec. Every number conveys global realities that even elude important decision makers. Learners can search their country and see a detailed profile of issues and problems.

**Environmental data** – The World Bank is an authoritative provider of tabular and graphical information about global environmental problems. Their site for this purpose is http://data.worldbank.org/topic/environment. The United Nations provides an Environmental Data Explorer at http://geodata.grid.unep.ch/. Learners provided with these links can search their country and ascertain the big picture, make relevant choices, and convey meaningful evidence using the statistics there.

Students are asked to find problems and solve them. This propels the activity to the top of Blooms as students brainstorm possible causes and solutions of a nation's promise or peril. By the end of this lesson, learners have created an evidence-based claim and are ready to argue for funding to solve their country's real-world problem. As they plead for those in power to address their issue, they have reached the top of Blooms and beyond.

Each ambassador should be ready and able to use the vocabulary of the discipline to spotlight how they contribute to the world economy, or why they are not able to. Knowledge products present alternative to former written reports.

| Lesson: | United Nations Summit |
|---|---|
| Learning Targets: | Students will examine a country to understand how strengths and weaknesses fit into a global economic picture.<br>Students will begin to understand the meaning of being "globally interdependent."<br>Students will explain how policies are developed to address public problems<br>(C3 Framework Social Studies Standards).<br>Students will use credible databases to investigate answers.<br>Students will practice speaking with text-based answers. |
| Essential Questions: | How can we use a credible database to investigate answers?<br>How are countries dependent upon each other?<br>How do countries strengths and weaknesses affect their economy?<br>How does the topography, geography, natural resources and other factors such as population affect the economy of a country? |
| Text | **Books:**<br>Hungry Planet: What the World Eats by Peter Menzel and Faith D'Aluisio<br>What's for Lunch?: How schoolchildren eat around the world by Andrea Curtis<br>Material World: A Global Family Portrait by Peter Menzel, Charles C. Mann and Paul Kennedy<br>If You Lived Here: Houses of the World by Giles LaRoche<br>A Life Like Mine by DK Publishing<br>(And other books exposing different living conditions and concerns.)<br><br>**Databases:**<br>Kids InfoBit <www.gale.cengage.com/**InfoBits** )><br>EBSCO Primary Search <http://www.ebscohost.com/us-elementary-schools/primary-search><br>eLibrary <http://www.elibrary.com><br>CultureGrams: <http://culturegrams.com/><br>and others suitable for Grade 4–5, which will likely spotlight issues beyond surface facts such as holiday celebrations.<br><br>**Websites:**<br>URL's such as the US Department of State and those listed here will give real-world data on problems, warnings and other concerns.<br>http://www.who.int/countries/en/—World Health Organization will list health concerns<br>http://www.who.int/research/en/—Global health monitoring<br>http://travel.state.gov/content/passports/english/country.html (may be a rigorous read)<br>www.cia.gov CIA World Factbook—This site provides an lists issues and concerns<br>http://data.worldbank.org/topic/education#boxes-box-topic_cust_sec. Education Stats<br>http://data.worldbank.org/topic/environment. UN Environmental Data http://geodata.grid.unep.ch/ - Environmental data |
| Power words | Global interdependency currency, mortality, economics, government, opportunity, education, opportunity, borders, and others that may become your local focus |
| Vocabulary of library discipline | Keywords, evidence, investigate, claim, source, credible, inquiry, research, report |

| CCSS Goals | x | Vocabulary use | x | Solve real-world issues | x | Discuss, interpret, explain |
|---|---|---|---|---|---|---|
| | x | Nonfiction use | x | Research | x | Use formal English |
| | x | Close reading | x | Build and present knowledge | x | Rigor |
| | x | Evidence-Based Claim | x | Synthesis | x | Relevance |

| | |
|---|---|
| **Rigor** | This lesson uses data, information, and more to tap into a child's innate curiosity of their world. The EQ is difficult for an adult to answer and therefore will demonstrate the knowledge gained from all these activities. Low-level country reports are being "done" all around the nation. Most of the time these reports merely transfer facts found on the Internet or within an encyclopedia. However, this same subject matter may easily be transformed into a flat-world experience, which makes global concepts relevant to even a young child. |
| **Relevance Hook** | We indeed live in a flat-world—a globally interdependent world. The hook activity instantly instills relevance by asking students to record from home 15 countries of origin for: Clothes, food, and household goods. Students returning to school can represent that data in bar graphs as well as record frequency via colored "dots" on a paper world map. The paper world-map activity allows them the chance to visually "see" the concentration of world production and consumption. (Use different colored dots for food, clothing, and household goods.) It is likely that students will find many clothing dots are concentrated in China, Vietnam, India, and other "cheaper" locations. Food dots will likely be applied in Central America during winter months as well as many from within the USA. Household items will likely come from the United States, China, Korea, Malaysia, and other countries dominating manufacturing.<br>Our Inquiry endeavor begins with students' natural questioning ability. When "dots" are applied to the world map they visually indicate world economic activity. Inquisitive thinking should emerge as ten-year-old children automatically ask questions such as, "Why are there so many dots in China?" "Why are there so many food dots in Central and South America?" "Why do some countries have no dots?" "Why are we consuming so many items from other countries?" et al. |
| **Reader and the task** | The knowledge product for this research endeavor can take many formats. Examine the following and craft your own UN focused endeavor. Here are a few knowledge products and ideas that you could discuss with classroom teachers as an alternative to former written reports:<br>• After students research to discover the promises and perils of their chosen nation, they will need to synthesize this information to speak intelligently as that country's Ambassador. Each ambassador should be ready and able to use the vocabulary of the discipline to spotlight how they contribute to the world economy, or why they are not able to.<br>• Mock UN General Assembly with 'ambassadors' pleading International Monetary Aid to solve problems. (Evidence-Based Claim) Principals pose as the Head of the UN and award funding.<br>• Create a mock US Department of State website (Smore.com, wikis, Google Sites.), which spotlights problems and recommended solutions (i.e., the evidence-based claims of the collaborative group). |

| | |
|---|---|
| | • Create an infographic for the nation presenting your promises and perils and contributions to our flat world. (Piktochart.com or paper products)<br>• Each group can prepare a script for their UN Address and record it via Audacity. Students can collaboratively build a *Virtual World Map* with Thinglink.com hotspots on their country. These hotspots connect to Audacity recordings of their UN Address. If writing tasks are required as part of an ELA assessment, each student could write a persuasive argument paper building from the EBC that they constructed for their country. This could be done in the first person voice of the Ambassador or another representative that they have discovered to brainstorm their questions either in groups or collectively as a class. |
| **Assessment** | • The essential questions serve as pre- and post=assessment tools as student use the vocabulary of the discipline to articulate their conclusions.<br>• Graphic Organizer for creating an evidence=based claim. (Follows)<br>• Rubrics for presentation assessing: quality, critical thinking and original conclusions, use of carefully selected detail, and sense of audience and purpose.<br>• Formative assessment or planning and organizing a persuasive speech guides the process and the product.<br>• Student self-assessment bookmarks are recommended to keep students on task and help them pace themselves. Students would use these as a guide for finishing the task as well as insuring that the expectations are met. (See below.)<br>• Bookmarks for distribution serve to empower the students to mastery of the vocabulary of the discipline. These words may also be used to teach search narrowing: Major words and minor words—What are you looking for and what would you like to know about it? (Angola mortality; Pakistan sweatshops; etc.)<br>• Summative assessment rubrics used for "old" country reports can be modified to reflect the depth of answers to essential questions. |
| **Think Tank Spotlight** | This lesson embraces the anchor standard "research to build and present knowledge" and the close reading comes during investigation. Students are given choice and a voice in the knowledge product to transfer the learning responsibility to the learner. Students are asked to find problems, and human nature naturally tries to solve problems. This propels the activity to the top of Blooms as students brainstorm possible causes and solutions. By the end of this lesson, learners have created an evidence-based claim and are ready to argue for funding to solve their country's real-world problem. As they plead for those in power to address their issue, they have reached the top of Blooms and beyond. They have experienced these thinking activities:<br>• Inferring and reasoning<br>• Drawing conclusions<br>• Using thinking and not just experience<br>• Framing possibilities as well as facts, ideas without actual objects<br>• Developing complex thinking and view of the world<br>• Expressing personal thoughts and views, have intense interests<br>• Focusing on personal decision making<br>• Imagining outcomes of actions<br>• Calculating mathematically<br>• Solving problems<br>• Developing the ability to combine related items and classify them<br>• Generalizing<br>• Thinking creatively<br>• Beginning to monitor and control thinking,<br>• Planning |

| Blooms Barometer | Remembering<br>x | Understanding<br>x | Applying<br>x | Analyzing<br>x | Evaluating<br>x | Creating<br>x |
|---|---|---|---|---|---|---|
| **Standards Spotlight** | **National Social Studies Standards:**<br>• Construct maps to represent and explain the spatial patterns of cultural and environmental characteristics.<br>• Explain how the relationship between the environmental characteristics of places and production of goods influences the spatial patterns of world trade.<br>• Present a summary of arguments and explanations to others outside the classroom using print and oral technologies (e.g., posters, essays, letters, debates, speeches, and reports) and digital technologies (e.g., Internet, social media, and digital documentary).<br>• Critique arguments for credibility.<br>• Draw on disciplinary concepts to explain the challenges people have. faced and opportunities they have created, in addressing local, regional, and global problems at various times and places.<br>• Evaluate alternative approaches or solutions to current economic issues in terms of benefits and costs for different groups and society as a whole.<br>• Identify examples of the variety of resources (human capital, physical capital, and natural resources) that are used to produce goods and services.<br><br>**Common Core**<br>**ELA**<br>• Use precise language and domain-specific vocabulary to inform about or explain the topic.<br>• Refer to details and examples in a text when explaining what the text says explicitly and when drawing inferences from the text.<br>• Draw evidence from literary or informational texts to support analysis, reflection, and research.<br>• Explain events, procedures, ideas, or concepts in a historical, scientific, or technical text, including what happened and why, based on specific information in the text.<br>• Interpret information presented visually, orally, or quantitatively (e.g., in charts, graphs, diagrams, time lines, animations, or interactive elements on Web pages) and explain how the information contributes to an understanding of the text in which it appears.<br>• Integrate information from two texts on the same topic to write or speak about the subject knowledgeably.<br>• Draw on information from multiple print or digital sources, demonstrating the ability to locate an answer to a question quickly or to solve a problem efficiently.<br>• Speaking and listening standards: Discuss, interpret, explain, present claims and findings, use formal English<br>[© Copyright 2010. National Governors Association Center for Best Practices and Council of Chief State School Officers. All rights reserved.]<br><br>**Mathematics**<br>• Represent and interpret data<br>• Reason abstractly and quantitatively<br>[© Copyright 2010. National Governors Association Center for Best Practices and Council of Chief State School Officers. All rights reserved.] |

| Evidence-Based Claim: Show me the Evidence! | |
|---|---|
| **Claim:** | |
| **Evidence:** | |
| **Evidence:** | |
| **Evidence:** | |
| **Data:** | |
| **Conclusion based on research:** | |

From *Think Tank Library: Brain-Based Learning Plans for New Standards, Grades K–5* by Paige Jaeger and
Mary Boyd Ratzer. Santa Barbara, CA: Libraries Unlimited. Copyright © 2015.

## Self-assessment checklist

| Task Accomplished | Choose a country to represent as an *Ambassador* and prepare yourself to address the United Nations |
|---|---|
| | We have read about our country. |
| | We can identify real-world problems for our country and explain why we consider these important. |
| | We have chosen a few problems to investigate. |
| | We are listing strengths and positive points. |
| | We can identify keywords for investigating our real-world problem. |
| | We can read about our country and find evidence from databases and approved government sites to find facts, data, and evidence for our cause. |
| | We have identified a significant problem or two for our country. |
| | I can find credible information on my team's chosen problem. |
| | I can assess whether my information in credible, accurate, and usable. |
| | I or We have built an Evidence-Based Claim |
| | I am ready to argue why this problem needs to be addressed by people in power. |
| | I am ready to discuss our real-world problem with the class and have used evidence to support my claim. |
| | We are ready to use our power words our address to the United Nations: |

| Power Words of Country Reports | Power Words of Country Reports | Power Words of Country Reports |
|---|---|---|
| Ambassador | Ambassador | Ambassador |
| Border | Border | Border |
| Capital | Capital | Capital |
| Consume | Consume | Consume |
| Continent | Continent | Continent |
| Country | Country | Country |
| Culture | Culture | Culture |
| Democracy | Democracy | Democracy |
| Economy | Economy | Economy |
| Employment | Employment | Employment |
| Equator | Equator | Equator |
| Geography | Geography | Geography |
| Government | Government | Government |
| Inoculations | Inoculations | Inoculations |
| Mortality | Mortality | Mortality |
| Natural resources | Natural resources | Natural resources |
| Produce | Produce | Produce |
| Topography | Topography | Topography |
| Travel advisory | Travel advisory | Travel advisory |
| United Nations | United Nations | United Nations |
| Others I've found: | Others I've found: | Other I've found: |

**Country Report Makeover: Notes from the field**

As with any idea you read in this book, you are at liberty to use ideas and blend them with your local needs. One local elementary school has taken the time to makeover their country report into a year-long endeavor and shares how she wove some of these ideas locally. Liz Bailey, the local librarian at Okte Elementary School, Clifton Park, New York, and her co-teacher Karen Robbins, have implemented some of the higher-level thought we shared above and has taken her country report to the next level. Okte Elementary has a longstanding commitment to inquiry learning, and has pioneered strategies for the Shenedehowa Central Schools. Principal, Lisa Mickle, used learning communities to move inquiry forward. In Okte the students stretch their country report into a year-long *World Scrapbook*. Her poignant reflections below are a testimony as to how Inquiry-Based Learning yields deeper, expert thinkers and how you can use some of these ideas to improve what is happening in your school:

*Over the course of an entire school year, children in third grade conducted research to answer self-crafted essential questions in an inquiry learning project. Mentor texts, modeling, and library media mini-lessons guided learners as they explored the social studies strands in relation to several countries. The W.I.S.E. curriculum for inquiry learning (Wonder, Investigate, Synthesize, Express), was used to drive this long-range learning project.*

### How it was organized

*Every three to four weeks, students were given exposure to a new strand (geography, history, economy, government, culture, science and technology) through a teacher-directed group model using a mentor text, New Zealand. These models allowed children a shared experience to understand each strand in relation to how people live in that one country. This also helped children to understand our essential question, which was, "How does WHERE a person lives affect HOW they live"*

*For each strand, students brainstormed questions for library research that would apply to any county. Then they were assigned their countries. Two hours were devoted to this activity during each strand, and students understood that it was expected that essential questions were to be answered and understood for each student's country. Teachers assessed progress and provided guidance when needed.*

*Throughout the year, multiple information sources were introduced by the librarian, including atlases, encyclopedias, online databases and websites. Rather than being overwhelmed, this allowed knowledge of materials to be acquired gradually. Source introduction was carefully scaffolded so that children gained confidence and were able to see common features and usage similarities, allowing them to use nonfiction features effectively and independently.*

*The next step after research was the sharing of information in small United Nations groups. Each child brought key ideas to share about their chosen country within the same strand of social studies. During their UN conferences, children worked in consistent groups of 6 to take notes from each other. At the end of each strand unit, students participated in creating a small project to help express their learning. These mini projects included creating a weighted word picture, or Wordle, after the study of culture; or a bar graph in Excel after studying communication and transportation within the science and technology strand. This gave them a platform for sharing information as well as an opportunity to learn new technology skills.*

*A World Scrapbook binder was kept with students continually adding notes. The World Scrapbook binder was equipped with tabs that divided the year's work in an organized way, grouping continent countries together so that further comparing and contrasting would be encouraged, even after the year-long project was over. This created a culture of comparing and lively class discussions arose. The library media center had a special area called "headquarter," for conversations. During research time, it was not unusual to hear a student who had previously studied the same country giving information and coaching a student "new" to that country.*

*Our art teacher incorporated projects throughout the year to enhance children's understanding of world cultures, and those were added to the scrapbooks. For example, during one art lesson, a Japanese Gyotaku was created, which was an ancient way of recording an imprint picture in an advanced society before cameras were invented. A sense of pride and ownership of their own learning developed quickly in most students. Students even learned to use data to develop understanding of their countries. By the end of the school year, students were able to analyze how literacy rates, life expectancy projections, and technology access affects the way people live within their country.*

*The inquiry learning model lent itself to a very natural differentiation, allowing students to soar as they are capable, coached by collaborative instructors. Students with the Most of the class collected page after page of details to answer their essential question, when only one page of notes was required. Children who needed support were more likely to succeed with several adults available to guide the process. We stressed understanding over simply finding information to answer questions. Rich and rigorous databases such as CultureGrams, which offers an audio component that reads information on the web pages, were used heavily by students needing this assistance.*

*As with all student-driven projects, planning and preparing for this project was expended well before the year began. Nonfiction texts on about 30 selected countries from around the world with various reading levels to support all students were acquired. Many graphic organizers and student helps were created in anticipation of student needs at the third grade level. Student knowledge increased exponentially and their binders became thicker and thicker. Here are some of their comments:*

### *From the children:*

*"Now that I know more about the world, I understand more. I know some countries are rich and some are poor. . . I even know why some people don't have the freedom to read any books they want. . .I know that if a country's literacy rate is high, they value education. I've learned a lot about different countries this year."*

*"Next time I go to the public library, I'm going to use my World Scrapbook to help me find a book or movie so I can learn even more about the places in the world."*

*"Now that I know more about the world, it makes me inspired to travel around the world to SEE what I've learned, and also to see if I can learn even more about that country or continent."*

# The Battle of [*Cobleskill 1778*]                               **Grade 5**

"Can I bring my notebook home to make more notes?"

Fifth Grade Student

## WHAT IS THE BIG IDEA?

School librarian Laura Gagnon at Radez Elementary School, with community support, mobilized an historic reenactment of the local Revolutionary War Battle of Cobleskill. The fifth grade students transformed their interest in the war, sparked by the Schoharie County Historical Society, into a 15 minute, student written, documentary movie about the Battle of Cobleskill. The battle resulted in the burning of Cobleskill on May 30, 1778. Students researched, developed storyboards, wrote screenplays, filmed, and performed in the documentary. They created the maps, performed music, and wrote citations. A New York State award was presented to the librarian for her use of primary documents and archives.

The inquiry-based learning experience involved going beyond the walls of the school to a broad-based learning community. The Old Stone Fort Museum, located in the region, opened its archives to the student researchers and cartographers. Their educational outreach services facilitated student research during and after school. Letters written by George Washington, authentic maps from the time period, and an array of relevant resources sustained rigorous analysis, note taking, and planning.

This quest for historic accuracy, motivated students to reach back over the centuries and emerged in costumes of the period, performing period music, and marching the ground where soldiers skirmished in the 1770s. Using a shower curtain, student cartographers mapped the field of battle using historic maps and sources.

An army of volunteer community partners made this ambitious and student-centered project possible:

- High School Students in AV Club
- Parent as videographers
- The Stone Fort Museum
- The Schoharie Historical Society
- The Daughters of the American Revolution
- Music teachers, social worker, special education, principals, secretaries and bus drivers

This lesson could be replicated for any local battlefield in your area. Check out your local archives, museums and state libraries for sites that might work near you.

| Lesson: | The Battles of Cobleskill 1778- ELA/Social Studies Grade 5 |
|---|---|
| **Learning Targets:** | The students will be able to contribute in a way that is best tailored to their strengths. The students will be able to relate to their local history during the time of the American Revolution. The students will decide what characters are important to discuss. The students will be able to take ownership of their original creation. The students will learn real-world research skills and film/performance skills. The students will learn how to create a bibliography. The students will read and interact with primary documents. The students will see where history happened. The students will work as a team. |

| | The students will create an original thesis. The students will create a storyboard. The students will create a unique and useful project. The students will contribute to an encouraging environment. The students will build a learning community. | | | | | |
|---|---|---|---|---|---|---|
| **EQs:** **Guiding Questions:** | How and why did Revolutionary War history happen in our own town? How did the Battle of Cobleskill connect history, geography, multiple perspectives, and culture in 1778 and 2010? How can primary documents uncover the events and individuals connected with the Battle of Cobleskill? How can maps recreate the past with historical accuracy? Who left behind the primary documents that account for an event in local history? Who preserved the past in these documents? What dress, music, weapons, and features of every day colonial life need to be in a movie of the battle? How can a community collaborate to reenact the past? How does storyboarding and screenplay writing for a reenactment depend of research? How does technology enable the documenting of the past and the sharing of our work? | | | | | |
| **Text** | Substitute your local resources for those in [brackets] Primary and secondary documents regarding the history of [ the Battle of Cobleskill] Speech by the historian of [Schoharie County, New York] Archives of the [Old Stone Fort Museum near Cobleskill] Texts from libraries that sustained investigation of clothing, flags, music, and geography Letters [from George Washington] in archives Digital resources from the[ New York State Library and State Museum] | | | | | |
| **Power words** | Revolutionary , archives, cartographer, colonial, costumes, troops, mercenary, patriot, loyalist, neutral, Great Britain, militia, allies, King George, Iroquois Indians, Joseph Brandt, campaign, settlements, George Warren, Captain Brown, Captain Patrick, continental army, defensive, attack, musket, reenact | | | | | |
| **Vocabulary of library discipline** | Screenplay, DVD, investigate, primary documents, storyboard, note taking, main ideas, supporting details, evaluate, access, digital, preservation, museum, dialog, communicate, collaborate | | | | | |
| **CCSS Objectives** | x | Vocabulary use | | Solve real-world issues | x | Discuss, interpret, explain |
| | x | Nonfiction use | x | Research | x | Use formal English |
| | x | Close reading | x | Build and present knowledge | x | Rigor |
| | | Evidence-Based Claim | | | x | Relevance |

| | |
|---|---|
| **Rigor** | School librarian shared these points:<br>• Traveling to Stone Fort Museum with "researchers" as expert groups<br>• Reading, analyzing, and synthesizing primary historical documents<br>• Learning about the camera and film terminology<br>• Reporting to group<br>• Storyboarding<br>• Writing the script in the classroom<br>• Filming in the library and on the school grounds<br>• Recording the band<br>• Filming at the Old Stone Fort (with parent help!)<br>• Editing the video |
| **Relevance** | • Seeing how historians work<br>• Exposing students to new technology<br>• Working hard is rewarded<br>• Learning is authentic<br>• Building community<br>• Receiving positive feedback<br>• Appearing in the local paper twice<br>• Writing script and citations fluently<br>• Appearing on local news<br>• Building lasting relationships with each other and community<br>• Visiting the community<br>  Showing more excitement about school<br>• Sharing their DVD with the entire community |
| **Reader and the task** | The fifth grade readers were joined in a common purpose: recreate the Battle of Cobleskill on DVD. Their reading was focused and rigorous. Accessing historic documents written and drawn in revolutionary times, students deciphered handwritten records, took meaningful notes, and synthesized a sequence of scenes that told the documentary history of a battle that happened in their own town. Translating language from the 1770s, using vocabulary knowingly, and distilling the most meaningful details to support main ideas challenged these motivated historians. Further, they used what they read to create costumes, perform music, map the events, and create an archive shared with the entire community. |
| **Assessment** | Positive Student Feedback<br>5th grade banquet show<br>Positive feedback from parents<br>Appearing in the local paper twice<br>Students writing script and citations fluently<br>Students "above and beyond" interest<br>Appearing on local news<br>Students building lasting relationships with each other<br>Students visiting with us and other teachers in the community and<br>showing more excitement about school |
| **Think Tank Spotlight** | **Use open ended questions:**<br>What do you think, wonder?<br>What do you see? Feel?<br>What do you think happened? |

| | |
|---|---|
| | Why does that happen?<br>How can you tell?<br>Why is this different?<br><br>• Questions move from a groundwork of facts to HOW, WHY, SHOULD, WHAT IF<br>• Multiple perspectives enhance understanding, and factor into close reading and writing<br>• Multiple causes and multiple effects can be understood and manipulated<br>• Long-term and immediate causes and effects can be distinguished<br>• Change over time can be discerned and represented<br>• Relationships among patterns and processes are recognized<br>• Different forms of evidence are analyzed and used to construct meaning<br>• Integrating information from sources is increasingly based on evaluation of that information<br>• Support of opinions employs grouping ideas<br>• Reasoning is increasingly based on supporting facts and details<br>• Use of evidence from texts along with reflection supports research<br>• Self-awareness about thinking and learning develops<br>• Metacognition becomes more sophisticated and productive<br>• Focus is increasingly key to performance in complex tasks, writing, and communicating<br>• Linking ideas within and across categories employs language that makes distinctions<br>• Logic in ordering ideas increasingly demands reflection and analysis<br>• Drawing conclusions from information and knowledge is genuine synthesis<br>• Expanding and structured networks in the brain facilitate retention of new knowledge<br>• Organization of mental tasks becomes faster and more extensively used<br>• Prior knowledge makes new knowledge easier to store in long-term memory<br>• Subject area expertise impacts speed and continued new knowledge acquisition<br>• Memory strategies begin to support new learning |
| **Standards Spotlight** | **C3 Social Studies Standards**<br>• Construct maps and other graphic representations of both familiar and unfamiliar places.<br>• Generate questions about individuals and groups who have shaped significant historical changes and continuities.<br>• Summarize how different kinds of historical sources are used to explain events in the past<br>• Use information about a historical source, including the maker, date, place of origin, intended audience, and purpose to judge the extent to which the source is useful for studying a particular topic.<br>• Explain probable causes and effects of events and developments.<br>• Gather relevant information from multiple sources while using the origin, structure, and context to guide the selection.<br>• Use distinctions among fact and opinion to determine the credibility of multiple sources<br><br>**Common Core**<br><br>**Speaking and Listening**<br>• Include multimedia components (e.g., graphics, sound) and visual displays in presentations when appropriate to enhance the development of main ideas or themes.<br>**Reading for Information**<br>• Draw on information from multiple print or digital sources, demonstrating the ability to locate an answer to a question quickly or to solve a problem efficiently.<br>**Writing text Type and Purposes**<br>• Write narratives to develop real or imagined experiences or events using effective technique, descriptive details, and clear event sequences.<br>• Establish a situation and introduce a narrator and/or characters; organize an event sequence that unfolds naturally. |

| | • Use dialogue and descriptions of actions, thoughts, and feelings to develop experiences and events or show the response of characters to situations.<br>• Use temporal words and phrases to signal event order.<br>**Production and Distribution of Writing:**<br>• Produce writing in which the development and organization are appropriate to task and purpose. (Grade-specific expectations for writing types are defined in standards 1–3 above.)<br>[© Copyright 2010. National Governors Association Center for Best Practices and Council of Chief State School Officers. All rights reserved.] |
|---|---|

# CHAPTER 17

# THINK TANK STARTER KITS

**Time to launch lessons for your brain friendly library!**
Additional ideas are listed below to inspire you to build your own
Inquiry based learning endeavor with your teachers. Having read
this book, you are likely equipped to develop deep student-centered
learning endeavors from the ideas below.

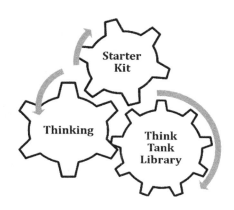

| Text or Content | Inquiry Lesson |
|---|---|
| Four Seasons Storyboard | K-1 emergent readers read, listen, and watch to answer questions with facts about animals of their choice, and how they live during the cycle of the seasons. The product is a four part storyboard with drawings of the animals in each season, and a THINK CAP Caption for each in the animal's own words. <br> Winter: "Here I am sleeping deep in my den with the snow outside." |
| What Snow Tracks Tell Us | K-1 explorers walk in the school yard and surrounding grounds to look for tracks in the snow. Using a cut out rectangular "window" they sketch tracks or take digital pictures. Repeating this data gathering, they research tracks in their area, and identify who is close by outside, walking in the snow. Students create a mural map of their school grounds with pictures of their winter visitors to match the photographs or sketches of the tracks. Finally they read, listen, and watch to draw conclusions about what kinds of animals spend winter in the neighborhood, how they survive and adapt. |
| Making Signs for Our Nature Trail | EQ: What signs could we make to enhance visitor's experience in our reserves? <br> First grade students take on the task of creating original signage for the one mile nature trail on the school grounds. Multiple ecosystems are found along the trail, and different habitats support different plants and animals. Scientific thinking engages and excites the |

| | |
|---|---|
| | learners who have the jobs of exploring, investigating, documenting, and designing markers along the trail. Each sign features notes about the ecosystem and the living things found there. "Look for a chipmunk gathering acorns under this oak tree." Old dead trees, wet areas, forest with a tall canopy, open meadow, and rocky outcroppings feature specialized life forms, adapted to that habitat. Birds, lizards, plants, trees, and rocks are observed. Research clarifies the important facts for the trail marker system. Original student drawings are generated for the trail markers with THINK CAP captions. Professionally produced metal and wooden signs are placed along the nature trail, each bearing the important scientific captions of the first grade planners.<br>Amsterdam City Schools, Amsterdam, NY |
| Freaky Frogs | EQ: Why should we care about our natural water resources?<br>A local pond has been featured in a newspaper because the frogs there have five or more legs, and the fish have too many eyes. What's going on? Students in grades 4 begin with details in the newspaper article, and extend their investigation to a Skype interview of a local expert from the State Department of Environmental Conservation.<br>With real world connections to Next Generation Science Standards, student collaborate to think like a detective and write like a reporter. Investigation of cause and effects of toxic dumping in the area, and letters to the town officials address a evidence based claim about a solution to the problem.<br>If you unfortunately have similar polluted water bodies, embrace this real-world relevant cause and effect science research project.<br>Science Standards: LS4.D: Biodiversity and Humans<br>Populations live in a variety of habitats, and change in those habitats affects the organisms living there. (3-LS4-4)<br>Make a claim about the merit of a solution to a problem caused when the environment changes and the types of plants and animals that live there may change. |
| Jack Prelutsky's Poem "The Mummy" | • This one page poem provides a backdrop to embrace academic vocabulary seriously. With 23 academic vocabulary words in this one poem, it is a goldmine to instill the value of learning valuable words to equip the learner for comprehension.<br>• Using the Essential Question, "How does Jack Prelutsky demonstrate his knowledge of Ancient Egypt in this poem?" gives your students motivation to read this poem a few times. In reading, they will encounter these words and absorb them into the receptive or productive vocabulary.<br>• The "task" to accompany this close reading activity could be a simple lesson on choosing keywords for searching, in order to answer your EQ.<br>• Keyword identification, Egypt AND mummies should yield information they need to provide evidence from a text, to answer the essential question. |
| An Octopus Is Amazing - By Patricia Lauber | EQ: How does the physiology of the [octopus] help it to survive in its habitat?<br>By choosing an animal set of books, each child can experience a "close read" to answer the essential question above. Or, your students can choose an animal book at their reading level to build an evidence based claim. First working within the text, the students read for details about their animal and build an EBC based upon the text.<br>This is a text-dependent activity, and then from there you can lead students deeper into an Inquiry activity where they go beyond the text to answer a larger essential question such as "How does pollution affect your animal's habitat. Or, what are the biggest threats to your animal's survival? What message will you deliver to the Department of Environmental Conservation? |

| | |
|---|---|
| Class Trip to Washington D.C. | EQ: How would a visitor from another country decide on American values and beliefs by touring the monuments of Washington D.C.?<br>EQ: How can we learn history from historic places?<br>EQ: What monuments are missing from our Capital?<br>Using the resources from the National Park Service Teaching with Historic Places Plans, students will wonder, investigate, synthesize and express conclusions about the monuments of Washington D.C.<br>Primary documents from the original planners and designers of famous monuments serve as a foundation for research. This will build background for their class trip. |
| Planet Reports | Low level planet reports can receive a "makeover" by transforming the knowledge product into a student-centered creative brainstorm.<br>Tasks such as these listed below will propel your students to new Inquiry heights as they :<br>* Write a script for an Intergalactic tour of the galaxy<br>* Create a multi-player dance to demonstrate the inter-planetary rotations of our solar system<br>* Create a script for a flying meteor, in the first person voice.<br>**Dance of the planets**<br>EQ: How do planets, moons, and sun in our solar system move in patterns around each other, creating day and night and changes in seasons?<br>Addressing the Next Generation Science Standard below, students create a knowledge product which is a dance. Students emulate the movement of the earth, sun, moon, and these things in relation to the solar system using scientifically accurate motion in relation to other bodies in space.<br>Standards: **Earth and the Solar System** The orbits of Earth around the sun and of the moon around Earth, together with the rotation of Earth about an axis between its North and South poles, cause observable patterns. . . . |
| Digestion: Inter-dependency of Body Systems | EQ: What happens to a [hamburger]?<br>Students choose their food and then complete an Inquiry research activity to plot the course of their food through their body.<br>Even deep differences between food and it's nutritional benefits should be folded into the answers. If, the students do not brainstorm these questions during the wonder stage of Inquiry, teacher's will serve as learning concierges asking critical questions to guide research: "What benefit does that ice cream have for you? Where will the nutritional vitamins end up? How do they help you?"<br>Posters, Public Service Announcements, Hamburger Journals and more can demonstrate learning. |
| Immigration | *The ELA novel, King of Mulberry Street* by Donna Jo Napoli pairs well with an investigative inspection into fiction writing with this essential question: Did the author correctly portray history in her book?<br>Students are required to research American immigration at the turn of the Century (1900), Ellis Island, European emigration reasons, and other NYC daily life details, to see whether the author correctly portrayed the time period, setting and characters in this book. Once again, with a vocabulary of the discipline bookmark, students are equipped with the tools to successfully wrap their head around essential building blocks of understanding and essential terms for testing.<br>The author could be placed on trial with collaborative teams presenting their evidence-based claims. This investigation successfully yields a student who has internalized the |

| | |
|---|---|
| | details of immigration, can speak with the vocabulary of the discipline, and who will remember the how's and why's of immigration for a standardized test. |
| Multiple Perspectives and the Revolutionary War | EQ: How did Patriots, Loyalists and Neutralists differ in their actions and attitudes before and during the Revolutionary War?<br>Students write historical children's books about a person or event during or before the Revolutionary War, effectively taking the perspective of a Patriot, Loyalist, or Neutralist in the narrative. Use mentor texts with perspectives on the war as models. Practice dialog in a debate between a Patriot and Loyalist.<br>Example: The Boston Tea Party, Benedict Arnold, King George, writing of the Declaration of Independence. |
| American Revolution- Pledge your allegiance! | EQ: Whose side are you on? EQ: To whom will you pledge your allegiance? King George or the New United States? Transporting students back to the 1770's, your students will work collaboratively to be representatives from a certain state, city, or village of their choice (from your list of 1770's real areas). Using this opportunity to teach research skills, you will ask your students to build evidence based claims and support either King George or our new United States. Knowledge products can include voices for their own "constitutional convention" or posters or newspaper articles for the *Boston Globe*, *New York Times* or *Philadelphia Inquirer*. By requiring someone to take the English loyalist view, children begin to build the meaning of perspectives. |
| Ecosystems through art and poetry | As a background building experience, inductively draw conclusions about the biology of multiple ecosystems by observing photographs, paintings, and drawings, and reading poetry that describes life in different ecosystems. |
| Biography Report | EQ: What indelible footprint did your person leave on the world?<br>EQ: How did your person change the world for good or bad?<br>EQ: Why did this person deserve to be inducted into our [hall of fame]?<br>Biographies are too often "information" products. By inserting a higher level thought EQ at the beginning of the assignment, teachers can focus the reading on a deeper learning adventure. Rather than Googling answers on the internet, students are required to think about the impact of this person's life.<br>By requiring appropriate quotes, and evidence from the text, a low-level biography report can be instantly more meaningful.<br>Knowledge products can include awarding high-impact awards, or living museums, but impersonators need to voice the impacts of the man, rather than factoids found in an Encyclopedia. |
| Classroom Constitutions | EQ: How does governing with the consent of the governed work?<br>Classes from early grades up can live constitutional government by writing, approving, implementing, amending, and democratically working together under a constitution for the good of the class. |
| Harlem Renaissance and the Jazz Age | EQ: How can the meaning of the Harlem Renaissance be captured and communicated using the music, art, and poetry of the time?<br>Students create collages, choral music, and a poetry wall to capture and communicate the Harlem Renaissance, after learning experiences in Art class with Romare Bearden, in music class with Jazz, and in ELA with poetry.<br>Hadley Luzerne Elementary School, Grade 5 |

| | |
|---|---|
| Dust Bowl | How can children survive when disaster changes their world?<br>Using the images from Dorothea Lange's Dust Bowl photography on the Library of Congress website, primary documents in the Dust Bowl collection for teachers at the LOC, and the non-fiction text *Children of the Dust Bowl* by Jerry Stanley, students build background to deeply understand the impact of the Dust Bowl on children and families. Concluding some of the ways children survived this disaster that changed their world, students will research Hurricane Sandy, tornadoes in the Midwest, and other life altering disasters affecting children. Knowledge products will address the essential question and become part of a composite banner about child survivors. |

# APPENDIX

In addition to the graphics provided within lessons, these additional tools you may find valuable for instruction. Use as you may to track brain-based learning. These tools are provided as samples to use with other lessons or while planning.

# EVIDENCE-BASED CLAIM EVALUATION

| Criteria | Comments and Scoring | | |
|---|---|---|---|
| | Strong | Good Try | Next time try... |
| Claim clearly stated | | | |
| Demonstrates your understanding | | | |
| Claim supported by text | | | |
| Sound thinking based upon evidence | | | |
| Uses direct quotations or text to support claim | | | |
| Explained thoroughly | | | |
| Includes vocabulary of the discipline | | | |
| Conclusion strongly summarized thinking | | | |

# Drawing Conclusions from Information

| Statement: | Inference – (hidden meaning) |
|---|---|
| | |
| Statement: | Inference – (hidden meaning) |
| | |

Conclusion:

## My Conclusion

_____
_____
_____
_____
_____

### Evidence

_____
_____
_____

### Evidence

_____
_____
_____

### Evidence

_____
_____
_____

### Evidence

_____
_____
_____

**How did I evaluate my evidence? Is my evidence FACT?**

**Name:**

| Claim or Conclusion: | |
|---|---|
| **Evidence, quotes, data, and other facts that support my claim: (indicate page numbers)** | |
| | |

# BRAIN TRACKER LESSON PLANNING

Teacher: _____ Grade: _____

Collaboration Connections: ☐ ELA    ☐ Science    ☐ Math    ☐ Social Studies    ☐ Art, Music, PE

| **Lesson:** | | | |
|---|---|---|---|
| **Learning Objectives** | | **Essential Question** | |
| Text(s) | | | |
| WONDER | | | |
| INVESTIGATE | | | |
| SYNTHSIZE | | | |
| EXPRESS | | | |
| Common Core Standards: | | | |
| AASL Standards: | ☐ Inquire, think critically, and gain knowledge.<br>☐ Draw conclusions, make informed decisions, apply knowledge to new situations, and create new knowledge.<br>☐ Share knowledge and participate ethically and productively as members of our democratic society.<br>☐ Pursue personal and aesthetic growth | | |
| ISTE Standards | ☐ Creativity and innovation<br>☐ Communication and collaboration<br>☐ Research and information fluency<br>☐ Critical thinking, problem solving and decision making | | |
| Brain Success | Social interaction | Rigor | |
| | Collaboration | Reflect | |
| | Chunking | Questioning or Socratic Dialog | |
| | Connections to knowledge | Solve problems | |
| | Emotional appeal | Relevance | |
| | Think aloud–metacognitive modeling | Synthesize | |
| | Deconstruct – construct | Variety | |
| | Choice | Original knowledge product | |

# BIBLIOGRAPHY & RESOURCES

Abbott, John, and Terence Ryan. "Constructing Knowledge, Reconstructing Schooling." *Educational Leadership* November (1999): 66–69.

"Adolecence." In *Encyclopedia of Psychology*. Washington, D.C.: Oxford University Press, 2000.

"The Adolescent Brain: A Work in Progress—Pat Wolfe. Mind Matters, Inc." *Pat Wolfe Mind Matters Inc.* http://patwolfe.com/2011/09/the-adolescent-brain-a-work-in-progress/ (accessed May 14, 2014).

Barahal, Susan. "Thinking about Thinking." *Phi Delta Kappan* December (2008): 298–302.

Black, Susan. "Teachers Can Engage Disengaged Students." *Education Digest* 69, no. 7 (2004): 39–44.

Bransford, John, Ann L. Brown, and Rodney R. Cocking. *How People Learn Brain, Mind, Experience, and School.* Washington, D.C.: National Academy Press, 1999.

Bruer, John. "In Search of . . . Brain Based Education." *Phi Delta Kappan* May (1999): 80, 648–654, 656–657.

Bruer, John. "The Mind's Journey from Novice to Expert." *James S. McDonnell Foundation.* https://www.jsmf.org/about/j/minds_journey.htm (accessed January 16, 2014).

California State University, Northridge. "2 How Experts Differ from Novices." http://www.csun.edu/science/ref/reasoning/how-students-learn/2.html (accessed January 5, 2014).

Chall, Jeanne, and Vicki Jacobs. "The Classic Study on Poor Children's Fourth Grade Slump." *American Educator* Spring (2003). http://www.aft.org/newspubs/periodicals/ae/spring2003/hirschsbclassic.cfm (accessed February 24, 2004).

"Childhood Years Ages Six through Twelve." *NC State University.* http://www.ces.ncsu.edu/depts/fcs/pdfs/fcs465.pdf (accessed February 11, 2014).

Choudhury, Suparna, Sarah-Jayne Blakemore, and Tony Charman. "Social Cognitive Development during Adolescence." *Social Cognitive and Affective Neuroscience* 1, no. 3 (2006): 165–174. http://www.ncbi.nlm.nih.gov/pmc/articles/PMC2555426/ (accessed January 13, 2014).

Chugani, Harry. "A Critical period of Brain Development: Studies of Cerebral Glucose Utilization with PET." *Preventive Medicine* 7 (1998): 184–188.

Ciardiello, A. Vincent. *Puzzle Them First!: Motivating Adolescent Readers with Question-Finding.* Newark, Del.: International Reading Association, 2007.

"Cognitive Development in Middle Childhood." *KU Department of Psychology.* http://psych.ku.edu/dennisk/CP333/Cognitive%20Middle.pdf (accessed February 4, 2014).

Cognitive Development, University of Rochester Medical Center. http://www.urmc.rochester.edu/Encyclopedia/Content.aspx?ContentTypeID=90&ContentID=P01594 (accessed February 20, 2014).

"College, Career, and Civic Life (C3) Framework for Social Studies State Standards." *National Council for the Social Studies.* http://www.socialstudies.org/c3 (accessed May 14, 2014).

Columbia University Teaching Center. "Transformational Teaching." Columbia.edu. http://www.columbia.edu/cu/tat/pdfs/Transformational%20Teaching.pdf (accessed May 9, 2014). "The Common Core State Standards

Develop Thinking." Center for Urban Education. http://teacher.depaul.edu/Documents/Common_Core_Toolkit .pdf (accessed March 21, 2014).

"Designing Inquiry Based Science Units." *A Community Approach for a Sustainable Growth of Science Education in Europe. Seed Cities for Science.* http://www.fondationlamap.org/sites/default/files/upload/media/Guide _Designing%20and%20implementing%20IBSE_final_light.pdf (accessed February 17, 2014).

Donovan, Suzanne, and John Bransford. *How Students Learn History, Mathematics, and Science in the Classroom.* Washington, D.C.: National Academies Press, 2005.

Duschl, Richard A., Heidi A. Schweingruber, and Andrew W. Shouse. *Taking Science to School: Learning and Teaching Science in Grades K-8.* Washington, D.C.: National Academies Press, 2007.

"Educational Psychology Interactive: Cognitive Development." Piaget's Theory of Cognitive Development. http://www.edpsycinteractive.org/topics/cognition/piaget.html (accessed February 17, 2014).

"English Language Arts Standards." *Home.* http://www.corestandards.org/ELA-Literacy/ (accessed May 14, 2014).

"Experts vs. Novices: What Students Struggle with Most in STEM Disciplines." *Arizona State University.* http://modeling.asu.edu/Projects-Resources/HarperK-ExpertVsNovice.pdf (accessed March 18, 2014).

Harada, Violet. "Empowered Learning: Fostering Thinking Across the Curriculum." *University of Hawaii.* http://www2.hawaii.edu/~vharada/Empowered.pdf (accessed June 9, 2009).

Harvard Univerity. "ALPS: The Thinking Classroom: Ways of Thinking." http://learnweb.harvard.edu/alps/thinking/ways.cfm (accessed March 29, 2013). Harvard University. "Artful Thinking." Project Zero. http://www.pz.gse.harvard.edu/artful_thinking.php (accessed May 15, 2014). Harvard University. "Visible Thinking." http://www.visiblethinkingpz.org (accessed May 2, 2011).

Harvey, Stephanie, and Anne Goudvis. *Strategies that Work: Teaching Comprehension to Enhance Understanding.* York, Me.: Stenhouse Publishers, 2000.

Hess, Karin. "Applying Webb's Depth of Knowledge (DOK) Levels in Social Studies." *NCIEA.* http://www.nciea.org/publications/DOKsocialstudies_KH08.pdf (accessed July 1, 2012).

Hess, Karin. "Applying Webb's Depth of Knowledge (DOK) Levels in Science." *NCIEA.* http://www.nciea.org/publications/DOKscience_KH11.pdf (accessed July 1, 2012).

Hess, Karin. "Applying Webb's Depth of Knowledge (DOK) Levels in Reading." *bllblogs.* http://bllblogs.typepad.com/files/dokreading_kh08.pdf (accessed July 1, 2012).

Hess, Karin. "Applying Webb's Depth of Knowledge (DOK) Levels in Writing." *NCIEA.* http://www.nciea.org/publications/DOKwriting_KH08.pdf (accessed July 1, 2012).

Hess, Karin. "Hess Cognitive Rigor Matrix & Curricular Examples." *PEDSAS,* http://static.pdesas.org/content/documents/M1-Slide_22_DOK_Hess_Cognitive_Rigor.pdf (accessed July 1, 2012).

Hester, Joseph. *Teaching for Thinking.* Durham, North Carolina: Carolina Academic Press, 1994.

Hirsch, E. D. "Seeking Breadth and Depth in the Curriculum." *Educational Leadership* October (2001): 22–25.

Hirsch, E. D. "Reading Comprehension Requires Knowledge - of Words and the World." *American Educator* Spring (2003): 10–29.

Hoberman, Mary Ann, and Michael Emberley. *You Read to Me, I'll Read to You: Very Short Stories to Read Together.* Boston: Little, Brown, 2001.

"Inquiry in Mathematics Supporting Kindergarten." *Saskatchewan Online Curriculum.* http://curriculum.nesd.ca/Supporting_Docs/Math_K/Inquiry%20in%20Mathematics.pdf (accessed May 13, 2011).

Intel. "Designing Effective Projects: Thinking Skills Frameworks Marzano's New Taxanomy." *Marzano's New Taxanomy.* http://download.intel.com/education/Common/in/Resources/DEP/skills/Marzano.pdf (accessed April 12, 2013).

Jaeger, Paige. "Repackaging Research." *School Library Monthly* September/October (TBP, 2014).

Jaeger, Paige. "Think, Jane, Think. See Jane Think. Go, Jane. Metacognition and Learning in the Library." *Library Media Connection* 26, no. 3 (2007): 18–21.

Johnson, Ben. *Teaching Students to Dig Deeper: The Common Core in Action.* Larchmont: Eye on Education, 2013.

Johnson, Doug. "Right Brain Skills and the Media Center." *American Library Association.* http://www.ala.org/aasl/aaslpubsandjournals/knowledgequest/kqwebarchives/v35/354/354johnson (accessed July 16, 2008).

"The Journey from Novice to Expert." *When Knowing Matters.* http://www.whenknowingmatters.com/the-journey-from-novice-to-expert/ (accessed January 16, 2014).

King, F. J., Ludwika Goodson, and Faranak Rohani. "Higher Order Thinking Skills." *Center for Advancement of Learning and Assessment.* http://www.cala.fsu.edu/files/higher_order_thinking_skills.pdf (accessed October 18, 2012).

Krynock, Karoline, and Louise Robb. "Problem Solved: How to Coach Cognition." *Educational Leadership* November (1999): 29–32.

Kuhlthau, Carol Collier, Ann K. Caspari, and Leslie K. Maniotes. *Guided Inquiry Learning in the 21st Century.* Westport, Conn.: Libraries Unlimited, 2007.

Lackaff, Julie, and Cynthia Hoisington. "Scientific Thinking." *NCS Pearson.* http://images.pearsonclinical.com/images/Assets/WSS_5/Research_Summary_Scientific_Thinking_FNL.pdf (accessed November 25, 2013).

Levine, Mel. "The Essential Cognitive Backpack." *Educational Leadership* 64, no. 7 (2007): 16–22.

Marzano Center. "Common Core on a Mission—Marzano Center." http://www.marzanocenter.com/blog/article/common-core-on-a-mission/ (accessed February 27, 2014).

"Mathematics Standards." *Home.* http://www.corestandards.org/Math/ (accessed May 12, 2014).

"Metacognition." http://www.etc.edu.cn/eet/Articles/metacognition/start.htm (accessed January 3, 2014).

Missouri department of Elementary and Secondary Education. "Research and Proven Practices." *MSTA.* http://www.msta.org/wp-content/uploads/2013/08/eq-ees-resources.pdf (accessed February 11, 2014).

The National Academy of Sciences. How People Learn. Brain, Mind, Experience, and School: Expanded Edition. http://www.nap.edu/openbook.php?record_id=9853&page=31 (accessed January 3, 2014).

National Governors Association Center for Best Practices and Council of Chief State School Officers. "Common Core State Standards Initiative." Home. http:www.corestandards.org (accessed June 14, 2011).

NCTE. "NCTE Framework for 21st Century Curriculum and Assessment." *NCTE Comprehensive News.* http://www.ncte.org/governance/21stcenturyframework (accessed February 21, 2012).

NEA. "12 Principles for Brain-Based Learning." *National Education Association.* http://edweb.sdsu.edu/people/cmathison/armaitiisland/files/BBLrngPrin.pdf (accessed November 20, 2013).

NEA. "Brain Development in Young Adolescents." *National Education Association.* http://www.nea.org/tools/16653.htm (accessed January 13, 2014).

"The Next Generation Science Standards | Next Generation Science Standards." The Next Generation Science Standards | Next Generation Science Standards. http://www.nextgenscience.org/next-generation-science-standards (accessed May 13, 2014).

Newmann, Fred, and Gary Wehlage. "Five Standards of Authentic Instruction." *Educational Leadership* April (1993): 8–12.

Novak, Katie. *UDL Now! A Teacher's Monday-Morning Guide to Implementing Common Core Standards Using Universal Design for Learning.* Wakefield, Massachusetts: CAST Publishing Company, 2014.

"The Novice Brain." The eLearning Coach. http://theelearningcoach.com/learning/the-novice-brain/ (accessed December 21, 2013). Odell Education. "Unit 2: Making Evidence-Based Claims—Odell Education." Odell Education RSS2. http://odelleducation.com/making-ebc-lesson (accessed October 23, 2013).

Partnerships for Assessment of Readiness for College and Careers. "ARCC Model Content Frameworks English Language Arts/Literacy." *Parcconline.* http://www.parcconline.org/sites/parcc/files/PARCCMCFELALiteracy August2012_FINAL.pdf (accessed February 18, 2013).

Pink, Daniel. *A Whole New Mind.* New York: Riverhead Books, 2005.

Railsback, Jennifer. "Project=Based Instruction: Creating Excitement for Learning." *Northwest Regional Laboratory.* http://educationnorthwest.org/webfm_send/460 (accessed August 5, 2012).

Ritchhart, Ron, and David Perkins. "Making Thinking Visible." *Educational Leadership* 65, no. 5 (2008): 57–61. http://www.visiblethinkingpz.org/VisibleThinking_html_files/06_AdditionalResources/makingthinkingvisibleEL.pdf (accessed January 19, 2009).

Savoie, Joan, and Andrew Hughes. "Problem-Based Learning as Classroom Solution." *Educational Leadership* November (1994): 54–57.

Small, Gary W., and Gigi Vorgan. *iBrain: Surviving the Technological Alteration of the Modern Mind.* New York: Collins Living, 2008.

Southwest Educational Development Laboratory. "SEDL - SCIMAST Classroom Compass." *How Can Research on the Brain Inform Education.* http://www.sedl.org/scimath/compass/v03n02/brain.html (accessed March 11, 2014).

Tate, Marcia L. *Worksheets Don't Grow Dendrites: 20 Instructional Strategies that Engage the Brain.* Thousand Oaks, Calif.: Corwin Press, 2003.

Tishman, Shari. "The Object of their Attention." *Educational Leadership* 65, no. 5 (2008): 44–46. http://www.ascd.org/publications/educational-leadership/feb08/vol65/num05/The-Object-of-Their-Attention.aspx (accessed January 17, 2009).

Tishman, Shari, and Patricia Palmer. "Visible Thinking." *Leadership Compass.* http://www.visiblethinkingpz.org/VisibleThinking_html_files/06_AdditionalResources/VT_LeadershipCompass.pdf (accessed April 28, 2013).

Twenge, Jean M. *Generation Me: Why Today's Young Americans Are More Confident, Assertive, Entitled—and More Miserable Than Ever Before.* New York: Free Press, 2006.

Vanderbilt University. "How People Learn, The Nature of Expertise." *CFT RSS.* http://cft.vanderbilt.edu/guides sub-pages/how-people-learn/ (accessed December 21, 2013).

"Virtual Information Inquiry: Pathways to Knowledge" *Virtual Information Inquiry: Student Information Scientists and Instructional Specialists in the Learning Laboratory.* http://virtualinquiry.com/ (accessed December 21, 2013).

Washington State Department of Early Learning. "Washington State Early Learning and Development Guidelines." *Department of Early Learning Page.* http://www.del.wa.gov/development/guidelines/ (accessed February 9, 2014).

Willingham, Daniel. "Inflexible Knowledge: The First Step to Expertise." *American Educator* Winter (2002): 31–49.

Willingham, Daniel. "Why Students Think They Understand—When They Don't." *American Educator* Winter (2004). http://www.aft.org/newspubs/periodicals/ae/winter0304/willingham.cfm (accessed February 24, 2004).

Wolfe, Patricia. *Brain Matters: Translating Research into Classroom Practice,* 2nd Edition. Alexandria, Virginia: ASCD, 2010.

Worth, Karen. "Science in Early Childhood Classrooms: Content and Process." *SEED Papers* Fall (2010): 1–11. http://ecrp.uiuc.edu/beyond/seed/worth.html (accessed April 12, 2014).

Wunderlich, Khaki, Annette Bell, and Lisa Ford. "Improving Learning Through Understanding of Brain Science Research." *Learning Abstracts* 8, no. 1 (2005): 41–43.

# INDEX

# ABOUT THE AUTHORS

PAIGE JAEGER delivers professional development at the local, state, and national levels and is currently serving on the AASL Task Force for the Common Core. Previously, she was a library administrator serving 84 school libraries in New York. Her published works include Libraries Unlimited's *Rx for the Common Core: Toolkit for Implementing Inquiry Learning* and articles in *School Library Journal, School Library Monthly, Library Media Connection,* and AASL's *Knowledge Quest on the C3 Frameworks for Social Studies State Standards.* She holds a certificate of advanced study and a master's degree in library science.

MARY BOYD RATZER is a professional development consultant who fosters inquiry-based learning and real-world strategies for the Common Core. Formerly she served as a teacher and school librarian at the Shenendehowa Central Schools in New York, and taught curriculum as an adjunct faculty at UAlbany's Graduate School of Information Studies. Her published works include Libraries Unlimited's *Rx for the Common Core: Toolkit for Implementing Inquiry Learning* and the American Association of School Librarians' (AASL) *Knowledge Quest on the C3 Frameworks for Social Studies State Standards.* Ratzer holds a master's degree in library science and a master's degree in the arts.

Made in the USA
Middletown, DE
09 September 2019